HIPPOCRATIC OATH

The man who died twice
and other stories

Also by the author:

Firing Neurons

Living Lines Are Never Straight

Hippocratic Oath

The Man Who Died Twice
and other stories

Barbara Orłowska-Westwood

The following stories and poems, including earlier versions, have been previously published as detailed below:

Stories:
Taste of Dirt (online Winning Writers, US), *Goodbye Doctor* (Lighstream), *On Duty* (Light Fals), *I Couldn't Do Anything* (That Untraveled World), *The Man Who Died Twice* (The Place Of Rest), *Don't Throw A Stone At Them* (under Polish title '50 lat pod znakiem Esculapa I Przysiegi Hipokratesa', Poland)

Poems:
To My Son (Red Weather US), *Lazarus* (Ulitaria), *It's A Boy* (*Disarmed* by Poetica Christi), *Living Lines Are Never Straight* (the book under the same title), *Visit To Pawiak* (Mud, Wind and Rain), *The Wedge* (Scant Journal)

Front cover artwork © Joorart.com

Typeset and printed in Australia by BookPOD

ISBN: 978-0-6489700-2-6   eISBN: 978-0-6489700-3-3

A catalogue record for this book is available from the National Library of Australia

To my patients

Contents

Time and Memory

It is a pleasure indeed to recommend the stories brought together in Barbara Orłowska-Westwood's collection, *Hippocratic Oath*. Based closely on her own experience, first as a young girl in Poland in the early years of World War II, in "Taste of Dirt," and then presenting details from the period of her medical training as a young woman and her work as a doctor in post-war Poland, the stories are remarkable compositions. Not only do they bring selected memories to life, on the page, but they also demonstrate, in the process, the writer's very fine care for language, stylistics and story-telling.

Valuable as an historical document for what it reveals about specific events in time and place, the collection is also intriguing as a very successful literary achievement. The first-person narratives combine the immediacy of lived experience, as it were, focused upon the girl, then the young woman in medical training and her practice as a doctor, with the invisible yet omnipresent guiding hand of the writer, the one looking back selectively upon past experience in an exercise of memory that is also, necessarily, evaluative as well as moving. At every point there are writerly decisions to be made about language and composition, inclusions and omissions, and always the interplay of particular characters and events with the wider contexts of family, social-political issues and the encompassing natural environment. These are important and they are handled very skillfully in this collection. The contextual details are presented economically. Often dramatic, as in references to war, soldiers, suffering and death, or with respect to medical systems, the institutions and demands of daily practice, they may also have elements of humour as well as anxiety and compassion. In this series, so much depends upon presentation of the narrator, Basia, whose voice we hear, and she is realized wonderfully as a figure of warmth, determination, awareness and charm, above all of sensitivity, one curious as a student, eager to succeed in her medical training even to the extent of bargaining for a skull, and competent in facing the challenges of medical practice in institutions and circumstances that are so often difficult as well as rewarding.

Complete in themselves, the stories are also glimpses that come together, much like the pattern of a discontinuous novel, while prefiguring further and other moments and events that might have been selected. Basia's history invites riches of association; her experience in dealing with delicate matters of gender, abortion, medical conditions, and tragedy is presented in ways, in contexts, that also suggest others, symbolic and real markers in the human condition. Some of this scope is implicit, for example, in the inclusion of step-father Stefan's voice, his experience as a doctor, including 1939, Poland occupied, terrors of war, a military hospital and his treatment of a former SS man. The final story, "Quiet Funeral," is Stefan's funeral, his wife and daughter attending to details, however modestly, images of the cemetery, band men in dark uniforms, their instruments, the surrounding trees, and sounds of Chopin together with the final moving image of Dad remembered at the piano. For lyricism, and for life detail and the Polish context, this short piece evokes aspects of the opening story, "Taste of Dirt," a little girl's perspective with her sensitivity to nature, family and then war, the appearance of soldiers and, significantly, her father's uniform.

Hippocratic Oath is a very impressive collection. The stories are short but, such is the poetic quality of Barbara Westwood's writing, they contain so much more than might, at first, seem obvious. Precise, lyrical, richly metaphoric, her language invites reading through the processes of association. The frames are multiple, the connections evocative, and, with particular history at its fingertips, the collection's reach exceeds its grasp.

Dr Brian Edwards

Taste of Dirt

When I was a child
the world went mad
standing on its head
it shook dark and evil forces
from secret pockets

I was four. It was autumn, harvest time. In the orchard the branches of trees, heavy with ripe fruit, hung close to the ground. Apples, pears, plums warm from the sun were within reach of my hand. Smell of honey. Bees flew around red and yellow asters, their buzzing loud in the silence of late afternoon.

And then, I heard my mother's voice calling from the house, 'Come here, to say goodbye to Dad. He is leaving.'

I ran onto the verandah. He stood there in his officer's uniform, tall and straight like the soldiers I had seen in photographs. He was different but when he smiled and lifted me from the ground it was my same dad. Only the fabric of his clothes was rough on my skin, and he smelled of new leather.

He put me down on the floor and I saw my mother crying, my grandpa and my grandma were crying, and my aunt cried as well, and nobody talked. And then my father turned towards the door. I saw the back of his head, his cap, green uniform, and the flash of light caught by his tall officer's boots. And he was gone. From the front of the house came the noise of the starting motorcar. It revved and was gone. Only the dust hung for a long time in the still air.

When the first bomb exploded in the town near us we were in the cellar. It was a small room under the house, cold and dark with cobwebs hanging from the ceiling, a storeroom for preserves, smoked meat, cheeses, empty jars and bottles. We sat there on the concrete floor. My mother hugged me close to her body, my head buried in her thick coat, her hand over my other ear.

First from the distance, later closer and closer we heard the roar of the planes and next the hissing screaming noise of bombs. I felt my mother's arm squeezing me and then came the explosion, and the silence. Only the jars and bottles on the shelves rattled, the dust settled on our faces, and I tasted dirt in my mouth.

> *Meadows were bright*
> *with wildflowers*
> *but on that fragrant carpet*
> *some gave their lives*

Every day of the school holidays I met Janek in our secret place. It was a little creek on the edge of the forest. The willows spread their branches across the water catching one another with their twisted limbs. It was our hanging bridge. Below it, in the filtered sun, the water ran fast over polished pebbles. It felt cold on our feet warm from the midday sun.

We sat on the stones, waiting for the fish to come. They were little, appearing suddenly like a cloud of silver commas only to swim away when we tried to catch them.

That day we were lucky, and we already had a few in our bucket but we wanted more. We sat patiently with our toes in the cool water, our backs to the sun. The forest murmured with the light breeze and from the fields came the fragrance of lupin in waves.

Our eyes were on the water, hands ready, when suddenly near us in the forest a machine gun rumbled. Like those fish that ran away from us, without a word we grabbed our bucket and holding hands ran towards my house.

Three days later when we met again at our secret place, we saw that near one of the willows had grown a grave. A birch cross, white in the sun, cast a shadow on the fresh dirt and a bunch of wildflowers left by someone.

> *Yellow chickens*
> *were hatching*
> *while on concrete streets*
> *black Gestapo uniforms*
> *spoke death*

'We are going to the town, your grandpa needs a few things', my mother said when she called me from the yard where I was playing with the dogs. We were soon in the carriage and driving towards the little town a few kilometres away from our property.

The first snow covered the fields, and the world was white and quiet. The naked trees stood alongside the road, black against the snow. Sometimes a shower of snowflakes came from under the horse's hooves. The snow swirled in the clear air to settle on our faces, clothes, and the sides of the carriage.

Dressed in a warm coat, hat, and gloves I sat patiently watching the ice crystals dancing in the air and shining on the horses' backs. I licked from my lips the flakes that were melting there.

When we arrived in front of the general store and were getting out of the carriage a group of German soldiers marched on the road. They led four men. They were Polish, in torn clothes. Blood was on their faces, their hands tied behind their backs. The Germans pushed them with their machineguns, shouting *Schneller, Schneller.* I knew it meant faster.

My mother said, 'Don't look, don't look,' and she covered my eyes with her hand. I still could hear the Germans' shouts and the sound of their heavy boots on the cobblestones. I smelled my mother's perfume but there was another smell around us, the smell of fear. Like smoke it clung to my skin and made it turn to goose pimples. I held my breath afraid to move.

When they had passed us, my mother took away her hand from my eyes. 'We can go now,' she said.

I saw the Germans disappearing behind the corner of the street and now Polish people, women and a few children, were running toward that corner. The women cried and they were pulling the children with them.

We went straight to the shop. My mother did her shopping, and I got my favourite sweets, which were like fruit jelly covered in icing sugar.

We left the shop and were on our way to the carriage when my mother stopped, grabbed my hand and pulled me back to the shop. From the corner of my eye, I saw on the street a German soldier in a black uniform with the letters SS on his arm. He held a small child wrapped in rags. Before my mother pushed me inside the shop I had a glimpse of black hair and the face of a child, a face darker than mine. Through the noise of a shutting shop door came the sound of a single shot.

'It was a Gypsy girl', said the shopkeeper. 'I saw that soldier chasing her on the street some time ago.'

After a few minutes we left the shop. On our way back through the town we had to ride on that road where the Germans were before. We passed the corner of the street where the soldiers disappeared earlier, and we came to the little square in the middle of town. We had been there many times before.

'Oh, my God', my mother said and forced my head towards her lap, holding me firm. But she was too late. I had seen something tall in the middle of the square, something I had never seen there before. It looked like four tall wooden crosses. But the cross that stood in front of the church had two arms. The crosses in the square had only one arm and at the end of those arms hung people, long and dark shapes against the pale blue sky.

> *Wild strawberries*
> *were ripening in a forest*
> *fresh blood*
> *on the green ferns*

It was summer again and the fields of grain shimmered like gold in the sun. The first cherries tasted sweeter than ever, and the long days were for play with the dogs and cats and the dwarf chickens, that I got for my birthday.

That evening we were sitting at the table, having our supper, my grandparents my mother and my father. He had come back wounded. I sat at the end of the table with my Auntie, my mother's sister. She often played hide and seek with me. Auntie was my friend and I loved her with all my heart.

We finished eating and the adults were drinking their tea when the housekeeper called my Auntie to the kitchen. We were ready to leave the table when Auntie came back. She was crying; her whole body trembled. My mother rushed to her asking, 'What happened, Marysia, what happened? Tell us, please.'

'Janusz is dead,' Auntie said through her sobbing. 'The ranger brought the news.'

Later I heard the adults talking. They didn't realise I could hear them. Janusz was Auntie's fiancé. I knew he fought in the Underground Army against the Germans. Two days before that evening he had been shot in both legs. He had realised that his colleagues would not be able to escape if they were to carry him. So, he had shot himself.

Bedtime story read

my mother's kiss

but I awoke to the shout

of man with a gun

aimed at my father

Our house stood among the conifers, chestnuts, and acacias. From the front of the house, I could see the farm buildings and I could hear the distant muffled sound of cows mooing, horses' hooves clapping on the cobblestones, people shouting. Sometimes the rooster gave his call and the dogs barked somewhere near the kitchen. At night the house was quiet, only my parents and I slept there.

That night my mother wasn't there, and my father allowed me to sleep in their bedroom in mum's bed. I loved that room. It seemed huge, full of light and the scent of my mother's perfume. In the late afternoon the shadows of maple branches danced on its walls.

It was still dark that night when I awoke to the noise of men shouting. The light was on, but my father wasn't there. His bed was empty. In the doorways I saw two men, one in each doorway. They had machine guns, they both looked at me, the men and machine guns; I saw the black holes at the end of the barrels. I closed my eyes as if I was asleep. I didn't move and I waited for my father to come back.

I waited a long time. When he was back and the men were gone and it was quiet again my father explained to me that those people were bandits, who pretended to be a part of the Polish Underground Army. They had taken a cow and two pigs from the yard.

The warm summer nights
waited for lovers
In Warsaw
not Jasmine fragrance
but smoke was in the air
and darkness red
over the burning city

July 1944 was unusually warm. It was still holiday time for Janek and me and we swam in the river every day and played in our little creek. The dogs and cats were still there. We ran with them around the orchard, picking the red apples and plums sticky with drops of juice that looked like little tears. Sometimes we took a carrot and without much cleaning ate it, feeling the grains of dirt between our teeth.

Everything was the same and it wasn't. Somewhere around us were secrets. Adults talked long into the night, or suddenly stopped talking when we approached them, but I heard the word 'Warsaw' repeated, and once I heard the word 'uprising'.

Different people, I had not seen them before, were coming to our house. Sometimes they stayed for a night or two. They were mostly young men; sometimes there was a young woman with them. Often they had horses and carriages full of something, and they put those carriages in our barns. I saw the men covering the carriages with hay. No one could see them after that.

One day four of those young men were in our house. They must have come late at night; I saw them first in the morning when we had breakfast together. When I went to the garden there was a table under the big pear tree and another five men were eating breakfast there.

Janek couldn't come and I had to play alone. My parents stayed in the house all the time talking with those young men. Those in the garden I saw later sleeping on the grass, under the trees. It was hot and black clouds were crawling from everywhere. My mother said a storm was coming.

We were halfway through lunch, those four men still with us, talking and laughing, drinking fruit vodka from little glasses, when we heard a motorcar engine at the front of the house.

My father went out and after some time came back with three Germans in green uniforms. He was explaining something to them in German. They nodded their heads and barked something back and my father said, `Yes, yes, of course'. Those words I understood, and they were all near us.

I saw my mother getting very pale and there was sudden silence at the table. My father introduced my mother and me and the young men. He told the Germans it was my mother's birthday, and we were celebrating it with our friends. It wasn't true. My mother's birthday was three weeks earlier.

The Germans sat with us at the table and had a glass of vodka and we ate the dessert together. But my mother didn't talk much. She went to the kitchen a few times and she was still looking pale and somehow strange.

I remember, before we had the dessert, the young man sitting next to me whispered, 'Can you count?' When I whispered, 'I can', he said, 'Please, go outside and see if there are any more Germans in the car or somewhere around it, and if there are, count them and tell me later how many.' I said, 'Yes', and went to the front of the house.

But there was only one German soldier sitting behind the steering wheel. He must have been their chauffeur, I told the man, when I got back to the table.

Soon the Germans left. My mother went to the bedroom. She said she needed to lie down. I went to feed my rabbits and chickens. The young men stayed and had supper with us but at breakfast we were alone. They must have left during the night.

Later, I overheard my parents talking and my father saying that the young men had a carriage full of arms, which they were taking to Warsaw. They had been ready to fight those Germans in our place, and then we would all have been killed, my father said. But, fortunately, the Germans came only because they wanted to check if my father had delivered the grain to the German Army, according to the order.

A few weeks later the sky over Warsaw was red. We saw it day, and night, for a long time, and we could smell smoke when the wind was coming from that direction.

We never saw again any of those young people who had gone through our house that year.

> *That time is now sealed*
> *in history books*
> *but alive*
> *in my nightmares.*

Lazarus

For my father and those murdered in Katyn Forest[*]

You were there
among thousands of others
in that lost battle

Wounded, taken prisoner
herded into the cattle train
driven towards Katyn

'Bolsheviks, they kill Polish
officers,' somebody said
he knew, he was in the Revolution

You wanted to live
you wanted to fight
you escaped

Hunted in the foreign land
among the enemy
and unknown friends

…killed in the battle…
…lost in action…
…shot during escape…

---

[*]   Katyn Forest - the place in Russia, where over 4,300 Polish officers taken
   prisoners in 1939 were killed in 1940 by the Soviet Secret Police.

They listened, they cried
your wife, your parents
your four-year-old daughter

There was no grave
to take flowers
to leave tears

On that day
when you knocked on the door
we had no tears to cry

no words to say
only hands to touch
only arms to hold you
our Lazarus

The Skull

I wanted to be a doctor. It was a dream I had carried in my head since I was ten years old. Seven years later, when one cold morning in October 1951 I rushed to my first lecture at the Medical Academy in Lodz, I thought I was the happiest person in the whole world. But Professor Boski, the anatomy lecturer, soon changed that.

He was from the old school of believers in discipline and hard work. His lectures were as dry and boring as his skeletons. He never smiled. The students called him 'Poker Face' and he became the subject of many frightening anecdotes. The most frightening concerned the pass rate for the anatomy exam. It was less than fifty percent. In the months that followed, fear, like a poisonous weed, took root in my mind and I became depressed.

My anatomy classes were held in a building called the Anatomicum. Erected in 1879 in neo-gothic style as a prestigious trade college, the building had Gothic solidity and seriousness softened by the flowing curves of stone ornaments. It watched the busy street through the eyes of its many windows. The tallest of them, stretching over two storeys, still had its original leadlight. On the wall above it was a huge sign in Latin: RES SACRA MISER, 'A poor man is a sacred thing'. The sign was engraved in 1932 when the trade college became a nursing home.

Every time I walked through the gate towards the Anatomicum I read the sign and thought nothing was sacred in our everyday struggle to find food and clothes. I forgot those thoughts quickly when I faced the door with the black and white plate, 'Department of Anatomy'.

The department occupied the ground and first floors as well as the basement, which was locked with a heavy metal door and was forbidden to us. There, in big tubs filled with formaldehyde, were kept the cadavers of those who had died in the streets, in nursing homes or in jails and had never been claimed by their relatives.

Before every class those bodies were brought in the lift to the ground floor and placed on concrete tables in the dissecting rooms. They lay there in a vapour of formaldehyde, waiting for us. When we arrived, we could smell formaldehyde even in our locker room, which was at the end of a long corridor leading to the dissecting area. At the end of each session, lasting three hours, my eyes would sting, and my throat felt as if it was lined with sandpaper. I didn't realise my clothes, my hair, my whole body reeked of this chemical, until one day on the way home in the tram I noticed people sniffing at me.

Professor Boski's kingdom was on the first floor. He reigned there surrounded by polished bones and glass jars holding hearts, livers, and other organs. It was a rare event for the Professor to appear among us downstairs. His approach was heralded by a sudden silence broken only by the sound of his measured footsteps. Dressed in a starched white coat, he would walk from room to room, his right hand holding a pair of long forceps glinting in the harsh electric light. He stopped only when he had chosen his victim.

That day, six of us were working at one table. Zosia and Mirka were 'doing' the vessels and nerves of the legs, Iwona was assigned to the tendons and ligaments of a hand, Jacek was dissecting the head muscles, Bogdan and I were working on the chest. We concentrated on our tasks. Sometimes we chatted quietly or consulted each other if our supervisor was busy elsewhere.

We had been working for more than an hour when we heard the Professor's footsteps. We all cringed and kept our heads down. The footsteps stopped at our table. I tried to shrink, to make myself invisible. I could hear my own breathing. The next thing I saw was a flash of silver light in front of my eyes. Professor Boski's forceps dived like a hawk into the cavity of the chest I was working on. He pulled up something resembling dirty grey string. Two eyes, the colour of Damascus steel, cut into mine. Then the famous question, 'What is it?' broke the thick silence.

He always expected an immediate answer, in Latin of course. I could hardly hear my own voice, when I said, 'Nervus phrenicus', feeling the dissecting instruments sliding from my hands wet with sweat. Was I right or wrong? I watched his face. It retained the same hard, indifferent expression. After a moment, he shifted the gaze of his metal eyes without blinking, the forceps plunged the object back inside the corpse and Poker Face moved to look for other prey.

* * *

A few months passed. February held the country in the grip of frost, and heavy snowfalls blocked the roads and streets making our lives even more difficult. But I didn't think about it. My mind was focused on the up-coming partial anatomy exam on the head and its contents.

That Monday afternoon, Zosia and I were studying in a small room in my parents' flat. My stepfather owned the place before the war, but in 1939 the Germans had forced him out of the flat and the town. When he returned to Lodz in 1945 the flat was empty, except for heaps of rubbish left by the Germans. He often said he was lucky because he still had a roof over his head while so many families in other cities had lost their homes. Zosia's parents were amongst them. When their house was burnt in 1944 during the Warsaw Uprising, they left the city of Warsaw and moved to Lodz. They now shared a four-room flat with two other families. The flat had one bathroom and one kitchen. It was almost impossible for Zosia to study at her place and she often came to study with me.

'So many of those holes, grooves, promontories, what runs through them, what is attached to them. I'll never learn it,' Zosia sighed and put down her notes. 'I'm sure I'll fail the skull.'

'Me too,' I agreed, pushing away the book that lay open on a page with an illustration of a temporal bone. 'This is hopeless. I need to see real bones, feel them with my fingers.'

'But how?' Zosia sighed again. 'The last seminar on the skull was a joke. I had that skull in my hands for less than five minutes.'

In desperation we returned to our notes and the old second-hand anatomy atlas lying on the table between us, a battered veteran of many learning battles, with its pages stained and torn, some missing.

For some time, we loudly recited the Latin names of the bones, checking them with our atlas and trying to visualise the real bones and their anatomical position.

Finally, Zosia threw her notebook on the table. 'We'll never learn it without a skull.' She stood up and started to pace the small room.

'A break, girls.' My mother walked in with a tray of sandwiches and two mugs of warm milk. 'Enough! Your brains must be steaming. You've been sitting here for over three hours, chanting those Latin words like a mantra.' She pointed to our treasure, the atlas, 'Basia, please take this dirty book from here and you, Zosia, please do sit down.'

When I cleared the small table, my mother put the mugs and a plate of open sandwiches in front of us.

'Look what I have for you,' she said with pride.

She stood there, smiling, waiting for us to take our first bite. Waves of her chestnut hair caught the glow of the lamp's light. Her cream blouse, faded with constant rewashing, was freshly pressed. Red spots on a wooden ladybird brooch pinned to her collar shone like rubies.

'Mum, this is real roast meat! Where did you get it?' I couldn't conceal my surprise, reaching for the piece of dark rye bread with thin slices of cold meat and pickled cucumber.

'I thought you would like it.' There was a mischievous smile on her lips when she said it. 'I was lucky at the market this morning. You deserve it.'

We were too hungry and too busy eating to enquire further. How was it possible to buy such a good piece of beef? The mystery was revealed a few days later. It was horsemeat– but I never told Zosia.

* * *

Time was running out and our exam was only four weeks away. Zosia and I became increasingly nervous and frustrated. We couldn't talk about anything but anatomy and we kept dreaming of the skull.

It was seven-thirty on Tuesday morning when I opened the door to the lecture theatre in the Anatomicum. It was my turn to secure seats in the first few rows for Zosia and myself. From the back of the huge room, it was impossible to hear the monotonous, quiet voice of Professor Boski. There were five hundred and twenty-five of us that year and the big auditorium didn't have a sound system.

I took two seats in the third row and during the next thirty minutes watched the arrival of my fellow students. Their young bodies were wrapped in layers of cheap clothes against the winter chill, their faces hidden behind home sewn or knitted caps and scarves. Those still half-asleep walked straight to the rear seats. They could doze safely there for the next hour and a half.

At a quarter to eight the main door was flung wide open, and I saw Zosia coming in. She hesitated in the doorway but when she saw me, she shouted, 'Basia! Eureka, we are saved!' She ran up the steps. Her coat was unbuttoned, and the scarf made by her mother from old yarns waved behind her like a rainbow flag. The blue knitted cap slid from her blond curls that, wet with snow, clung to her face. Her cheeks, usually pale, glowed like a fresh strawberry.

She caught her breath, sat down, and whispered into my ear, 'I know where we can get a skull.'

I pulled back, watching Zosia as if I was seeing her for the first time. Zosia was an only child and a great pride to her parents. Bright and usually quiet, she worked hard for her good marks, but the recent prospect of failing the anatomy exam must have affected her greatly, and in the last few weeks she had become even quieter than usual.

'What are you talking about? Who'll give us a skull?' I whispered.

'I didn't say it was being given to us. He'll sell it, for half a litre of vodka.'

I raised my eyebrows. I couldn't believe my ears.

'It's a long story. I'll tell you later,' Zosia whispered, pointing her finger towards the doorway where stood Professor Boski. In the sudden silence that filled the lecture theatre he walked the few steps to the podium. Like a general in front of his troops Poker Face held up his right hand. It was a sign that he was ready to deliver his long monologue.

After the lecture we rushed to the Milk Bar, two houses down the street from the Anatomicum. Milk Bars were cheap restaurants, run by the state. They were open throughout the day and served sandwiches and simple hot meals made mostly of pasta, vegetables, and dairy products. Our favourite dish was white 'barszcz' soup made from fermented rye flour, onions, wild mushrooms, potatoes, and a dash of sour cream.

The desire for warm soup made us run faster against the wind, which sent flakes of snow inside our collars. The bar was in a basement. Stone steps as steep as a ladder led to a small room dimly lit by a naked globe hanging from the low ceiling. Close to the ceiling was a narrow window that ran parallel to the street pavement. People sitting inside the bar could see a parade of shoes and boots walking on the street.

'Come on, there's a free table, next to that old couple,' Zosia said, pulling me across the room by the sleeve of my coat.

We sat at a small table covered in faded vinyl. From our seats we could see the wooden counter and the little kitchen behind it. There was a smell of wet clothes, cooked cabbage and burnt milk. I thought about people who might have lived in that cellar in earlier times. Like characters in the novels of Prus, Balzac or Dickens, they would have been servants or prostitutes, or poor tuberculous tradesmen and their children. Their only view of the world could have been through that gap in the brick wall, a gap filled with a piece of glass splashed with mud.

'Basia, are you with me? Wake up! They've gone. We can talk.'

Zosia's voice brought me back to the table. We had been afraid to talk about the skull as the old couple sitting next to us seemed especially interested in our conversation.

'So, what's the story?' I leaned forward on my elbows.

'Krzysiek, you know, the one with the ginger hair from group ten.'

'You mean Mister Know-it-all?'

'Yes, him and his mate Henryk, the Handsome– they got a skull from a man at the cemetery, for a bottle of vodka.' She stopped, waiting for my reaction to such great news. But I sat there, stunned.

'From the cemetery,' I repeated slowly.

'Yes, the Old Cemetery.' Zosia happily continued her story. 'I saw it, I mean the skull. Krzysiek showed it to me yesterday. It's perfect. Only the lower jaw is missing. Krzysiek said they tried to argue with the man, telling him, it wasn't fair to give them one without a jaw when they had paid the full price, but the man only laughed at them and said, "This one or none". He was so drunk, Krzysiek said, that there wasn't really any point in arguing with him. So, they took the skull and went away.' She paused for a moment and added, 'And now they have it, lucky devils. I'm sure Krzysiek told me about that skull only to make us jealous. They think we'll be afraid to go there to get one.' Zosia laughed. 'They obviously don't know us.'

Zosia's enthusiasm and determination quickly overcame my uneasy thoughts about the prospect of bringing home a real skull, clearly taken from somebody's grave. The idea of a night visit to the cemetery and meeting with the grave digger frightened us, but Poker Face frightened us even more and we immediately started to plan our venture.

Zosia learnt from Krzysiek that the man lived on the grounds of the cemetery but was at home only in the evenings.

'There is no other way. We have to tell our parents,' I said.

'Why?' Zosia's voice lost its enthusiasm.

'Look, we can find some excuse for going out late in the evening but what about vodka? No one is going to sell it to us, and we don't have money.'

Finally, we agreed that I should talk to my parents first, as it was obvious that I would have to keep the skull at my place.

*　*　*

On the way home, I was nagged by doubts. Zosia and I were about to become 'cemetery hyenas', scavenging the contents of graveyards. Grave theft was often a subject of gossip and sometimes we read in the newspapers about people stealing ornaments and sheets of granite from unattended graves and small chapels. Everyone knew those small thieves followed the example of the biggest robber, the City Council.

It was a public secret that the base of the monument of Stalingrad Heroes standing in the biggest park in Lodz, was made from black marble taken from the Old Lutheran Cemetery. That cemetery had beautiful monuments and chapels built before the war by rich businessmen, mostly migrants from Germany. Since the defeat of the Nazis, the communist regime had treated the graves as enemy property and robbed them openly.

They are stealing, I thought, but we are going to pay for our skull, so it won't be theft. More difficult to suppress was my fear of the gangs of criminals and homeless alcoholics who gathered at night in the cemetery chapels. We could only hope that the grave digger's place would be close to the main gate and the street.

* * *

That evening at dinner my stepfather said, 'I hear that you and Zosia have been studying anatomy very hard. Which part is it this time?'

'The head. There's just too much to remember. When I get to the muscles, I've already forgotten the nerves and bones, not to mention the brain.' I spoke slowly thinking about the skull, gathering my courage.

'I know, the skull is difficult, but the brain is even worse. I didn't like it at all. I almost failed that part,' my stepfather said. He smiled one of those childlike smiles in which his face lost its usual serious expression.

Now or never, I thought, looking at my mother, to see if she was listening. I needed her help. 'But when you studied, I mean before the war, it was easier,' I said.

'What do you mean easier?' My stepfather laughed. 'Anatomy is the same, a skull is a skull, and a brain is a brain. Nothing has changed.'

'But you had a skull to learn on and I don't have one,' I snapped, and then regretted it immediately. It wasn't a good tactic.

'That's true, but now as you know well, we lack many things that we had before the war, things more important than a skull. You'll just have to make do. All your colleagues are in the same situation.' His voice had turned serious which wasn't promising.

'I know of someone who has a skull. He got it,' I stumbled, 'I mean, he bought it.' And without hesitation, I repeated Zosia's story.

The first to react was my mother. 'That man must be digging them up from old graves. He's stealing from the dead.' She spoke quickly as she always did when she was upset. 'And you, Basia, want to bring it home, I mean somebody's dead bones, you want to bring home! No, I don't think so. All this is macabre and disgusting!'

'But Mum, I'm sure he is taking those skulls from very old graves. You know, there is legislation that allows burying another body in the same grave after twenty years. You know it, Mum'. I tried to protest.

'To bury, yes, but not to dig up the skeleton and sell it for vodka.'

'Don't be angry with her, Lilka.' My stepfather took his pipe and his long sensitive fingers started to fill it with tobacco. 'I agree, it's wrong to buy and sell skulls from the cemetery, but they're very old, as Basia said. There are many "younger" bones scattered over Poland since the last war. I'm sure we could still find skulls lying in the forests or buried in the fields.'

He stopped and puffed his pipe in silence, his brown eyes watching the darkness in a window's square. I was sure that in his thoughts he was back in the time of his own fighting during 1939 and, later, during German occupation, when death was such a common event.

After a few moments he smiled and said, 'I can understand your mother's concern, Basia, but I think buying that old skull will create less harm than risking the lives of your future patients.'

* * *

The following Friday afternoon Zosia came to my place. I had earlier put a bottle of vodka wrapped in newspaper into a hessian bag. The bag was big enough to hold a skull. We knew from Krzysiek that the cemetery gates closed at five pm. At four-thirty we were on a tram that went past the Old Cemetery.

It was already dark outside. Rain mixed with snow lashed the tram windows. People on the street, keeping their heads down and collars up, rushed to get out of the slush. The further we moved from the city centre, the more deserted the streets became. Finally, it was our stop. The tram door opened. We stepped out straight into a grey pool of water on the broken pavement. I tried to open my umbrella, but the strong wind turned it inside out. We heard the tram bell, the bang of the door as it shut and, before we knew it, the tram was gone, taking with it our feeling of safety. We stood there unsure of where to go.

Lost in complete darkness in front of us was the Old Cemetery. Established in 1857, it spread out over many hectares. To the left were the Evangelical, the Orthodox sections and a smaller part called 'communal' for those buried without God's blessing, such as known atheists, suicide victims and the homeless. The Catholic section was in front of us.

'We have to go to the right,' Zosia said. 'I remember, the main gate is further down the street.'

We started to walk, trying to make ourselves invisible, anxiously watching the empty street which ran alongside the cemetery wall. The old trees growing within the cemetery stretched their bare branches over the brick wall. They swayed in the wind above our heads like black twisted arms ready to catch us. We kept looking across to the other side of the street to the masons' workshops, where, here and there, a dim light framed by a window signalled that people were still around.

After a few minutes we came to the main gate. Through its ironwork we saw in the distance the outspread arms of the huge wooden cross which stood in the middle of the cemetery's main roadway. During the day people placed flowers at the foot of the cross and lit candles for the dead and missing in foreign lands. But now the cross's black silhouette rose from a sea of blackness.

Another fifty metres, and the brick wall ended in a small alcove in which we saw a timber gate. We had to push hard to open it. It screeched loudly in protest. The noise made me shiver. Behind the gate was a narrow path darkened by overgrown conifers. It led to a small hut. Through the torn curtain in one of the windows we could see inside the room where a naked globe hung down from a low ceiling. We stopped as if somebody had given us a command. We turned towards each other, and our eyes met. I felt Zosia trembling. I squeezed her hand. We are not going back, I thought, searching Zosia's eyes. After a few seconds without a word, we moved towards the hut and quickly walked the last few metres.

There was no response to our knock at the door. We tried again, harder. Nothing. Determined, we started to bang with our fists when we heard a man's voice call out, 'Who's there?' 'We would like to speak to the grave digger,' we shouted back. There was a moment of silence, then a harsh cough and a shuffle of unsteady feet on the wooden floor. The heavy door opened slowly, and we saw in the doorway the figure of a tall man in torn clothes stained with mud and clay. His face seemed covered by a dirty grey mask. I moved a step back but then realised it was a fringe of his grey hair coming down to the eyebrows and on to the side of his face where it joined the thick beard. The smell of boiled sauerkraut streamed out from the little room mixing with the odour of the man's sweat and stink of alcohol on his breath. He stood leaning on the doorframe blocking the entrance.

'What do you want?' he shouted, his eyes moving from our head to feet, going up again, and finally they focused on mine.

'We would like a skull. We are students from the Medical Academy. Someone told us'–

'What?'

'We would like,' I started again but this time I was shouting at him.

'Fine,' he said quietly. 'It'll cost you.'

I produced the bottle. His big hand grabbed it without hesitation. He put the bottle on the floor behind him, stepped out of the house and shut the door. 'Wait here.' He left us and walked in the direction of the black silhouette of a small chapel visible nearby. When he returned, he carried something under his arm.

'Here,' he stopped in front of us and stretched out his huge dirty hand holding a skull. In the dim light of the small hut's window the bones seemed made of a yellow wax. The skull looked at us with its black holes of eye-sockets. A few teeth were still in the upper jaw. I put out both my hands covered in thick gloves and took the skull.

'Thank you,' we said, pushing our treasure into the bag without bothering to wrap it properly in the newspaper. He watched us for a short moment then smiled an eerie smile and without a word went back to his hut.

We turned and ran towards the cemetery gate and into the street. It was empty and dark as before. We heard the rattling noise of the tram and saw its lights approaching fast, so we kept running towards the tram stop. In a few minutes we were among the people in the safety and warmth of the tram. On the way home we didn't talk, afraid that people would overhear. But every time we looked at our bag we smiled at each other.

Three weeks later we both passed our exam on the head and in June we gained high marks in the final anatomy exam at the end of our academic year. I decided to give the skull as the birthday present to my cousin, Ania. She had just passed her entry exam to the Medical Academy.

I wrapped the skull in layers of blue tissue paper, put it carefully into a box and tied the box with a silver ribbon. On the top of the box, I printed *fragile* and placed the package on the shelf in my room. It had to stay there till Ania's birthday at the beginning of August.

The Man Who Died Twice

It was 1953 in Poland. Our country was separated from the West by the Iron Curtain. It had been ruled by Stalin's protégées and was kept in constant fear by his Internal Security. Polish people, those who had fought in the allied forces or had been members of the Polish Underground Army*, were now on the regime's 'blacklist. Many of them, arrested under the pretext of previous 'collaboration with the Germans', were tortured and killed in Polish communist prisons.

I was half-way through my medical studies. I lived with my mother and my stepfather, a medical doctor, in the city of Lodz. I loved him and called him Dad.

In late September it was already dark outside by six o'clock. The light drizzle settled in for the night. Autumn with its wet and cold days was approaching fast.

Mum was ready to serve dinner when the bell at the front door rang. I opened the door. The man standing there was tall with light hair. His clothes were clean and bore the signs of frequent washing. They hung loose on his broad shoulders. The skin on his face had a leathery look, a result of previous exposure to hash weather, but in the light of the bare globe on the landing, he looked pale, almost grey. He was probably in his thirties but appeared much older.

He stood there turning his faded cap in both hands. His blue eyes looked straight at me when he asked, 'Is Doctor Kopczynski living here?' His speech was not clear, as if he had difficulty moving his tongue.

When I said, 'Yes', the man sighed with relief and something like a smile passed over his face.

'Thank God I finally found my doctor,' he said. Then he asked, 'Could I speak to him now, please?'

He must have seen my hesitation because he added, 'I know it's late but please let me talk to the doctor. He will remember me.'

I opened the door wider, 'Please come in,' I said, and let the man into our small hall. 'Please take a seat and I'll ask Dad to come.'

Both men disappeared into Dad's study. Mum said, 'I'd better put the dinner in the oven. I hope they won't be too long.'

We waited over an hour. When the man left and the three of us sat at the table for our late dinner, Dad told us the man's story.

'During the German occupation, as you know, I had to escape from the city and I was living in the ranger's house on the outskirts of the big forest spreading towards Warsaw. I worked as a doctor treating locals from the villages and neighbouring small towns. Sometimes I was called to treat the wounded, so-called partisans, members of the Polish

Underground Army, which was active in that part of the country and in that forest.

'One night, long after the curfew,' Dad said, 'the ranger came to my room with news that there was a wounded partisan in the village a few kilometres from his house.' Dad talked, looking first at us and then at the darkness beyond the window, as if he saw the events of that night there. 'I took my doctor's bag and my bicycle and with the ranger as my guide on the forest tracks, we set out for our trip to the wounded man. The house he was in stood alone, surrounded by forest. He was being cared for by a poor peasant family with four children. The house had only three rooms and a kitchen. In one of those rooms was this man. His body was covered with wounds, some superficial some deeper, alive with maggots.'

My mother and I stopped eating but Dad didn't notice it.

'You can imagine,' he said. 'It was a small room, and it was the middle of summer; it was hot. The stink in the room was nauseating. The man couldn't speak, his tongue was in pieces, and he had a wound in his soft palate. He had also lost a few teeth.'

'What did you do?' I asked.

'I couldn't do much apart from cleaning his wounds and filling them with sulphonamide powder as an antiseptic.' Dad paused and turned to me, 'There was no penicillin available yet for us,' he said. 'Anyway,' Dad continued his story, 'After I finished cleaning the wounds and saw the man's tongue there was nothing else to do except pray for him.'

'It took him a good few weeks, but he was young and strong, and he survived. His speech wasn't the best but when he was able to talk, he told me how it all happened.' Dad stopped, looked at my mother and said, 'I think I need a glass of something stronger than tea before I get to that story.'

'Was this the same man who came this evening?' I asked.

'Yes, this is the man,' Dad said and started to fill his pipe with tobacco.

When my mother brought us a cup of tea and Dad had a glass of brandy in his hand he went back to his story. He was talking to us, but his eyes had a distant expression. In his thoughts Dad was far away from us. He was back in that small, stinking room listening to the man telling Dad of his escape.

'He had been a member of a group of partisans that organized the attack on a small local jail where the Germans were keeping four Polish people arrested a few days before. Those people were important to the Polish Underground Army, but somebody had betrayed the partisans and they fell into a trap. Most of the partisans were killed, but a few were captured, and among them was this man. They were locked in a cell. Shortly after that the Germans threw several grenades into the cell. This man was wounded and lost consciousness. When he came round, he saw a German soldier in the cell, an SS man. He was checking to see if every one of the prisoners was dead. Those still alive he was killing with two shots to the back of the head. Our man was badly wounded but still alive. The last thing he remembered from that cell was the moment when the SS man put the gun against his head.'

'Later, the Germans ordered a local peasant to load the bodies on a horse carriage, take them to the nearby forest and bury them. The road was bumpy and slow and after some time our man regained consciousness. He realized he was still alive and among the corpses being driven through the forest. With the remainder of his strength, he slid from the carriage and crawled, as far as he could, from the road into the bushes. There he collapsed. He was found next day by children picking mushrooms. They were the children from the farm where he was hidden later.'

'How was it possible that he was shot twice in the back of the head and the bullets didn't injure his spine or the arteries?' I asked, picturing in my mind the anatomy of the human neck.

'I couldn't believe my eyes,' Dad smiled for the first time that evening. 'It was really a miracle, and if someone had told me it was possible, I would not have believed it.' Dad smiled again. 'But I saw it, and it was real. Both bullets passed through the neck and went out through the mouth leaving intact the major structures, but damaging his tongue, his palate, and a few teeth.'

For some time, we all were silent. My mother was the first one to speak when she said, 'You could say, he is the man who died twice.'

'He was very lucky.' Dad spoke slowly as if he wasn't yet fully back with us in our city flat.

'Why did he come this evening? He was so relieved when he learnt that he had found you,' I said looking at Dad.

The smile disappeared from Dad's face and there was a note of anger in his voice when he said, 'The usual story. Last year he was arrested by our Internal Security and put into jail. They kept him for a few months and finally charged him with collaboration with Germans during the Occupation. His solicitor gathered some witnesses who were still alive and got the man released, but the court process is still hanging over him. Since his release he has been looking for me hoping that I would still remember him. He needed a certificate from me for the court, stating that I treated him years ago from the wounds he sustained fighting the Germans.'

Dad's pipe had long stopped smoking and now he shook the ash out of it into the ashtray. My mother and I watched the movements of his fingers – every one of us deep in our own thoughts.

'It's late, almost twelve o'clock.' My mother as always brought us back to reality. 'We can't change anything. We know that they can do to us whatever they want. Thinking about it can only bring us more frustration and make us ill.' She got up and collected our empty cups.

'I'll help you wash the dishes,' I said.

When we left the room Dad was still sitting at the table. He was looking at the dark panel of the window. The empty pipe was still in his hand.

* Polish Underground Army, also called Home Army, during the German occupation was connected to the Polish Government on Exile in London.

Visit to *Pawiak*[*]

Brick walls
soaked with blood, pain, despair
black metal
twisted, tortured into odd shapes
the dark stump of a tree
covered with white metal plaques
every plaque somebody's life
cut down like this tree

their dreams, loves, expectations
ended here
when they were only
twenty-one, sixteen, fourteen, twenty-five…
so much waste, so much sacrifice
and we stand here in silence
remembering

[*]   *Pawiak* – A jail in Warsaw. During 1939-1945 it was one of main
     jails used by Gestapo in which 30 thousand out of 90 thousand
     prisoners were murdered. There is now a Museum and a Monument of
     Martyrdom on the site.

Don't Throw a Stone at Them

It is October 1951. I stand in front of the full-length mirror in my mother's bedroom. In the glass I see a seventeen-year-old girl in a doctor's white coat. I smile at her. 'Doctor Barbara Wislawska', I say aloud.

Then in the mirror next to me I see my mother's face with a big smile on her lips. 'My little girl', she says putting her arms around me. We stand in this embrace for a long moment. I feel the warmth of her body, the softness of her palm when she strokes my cheek. 'My little girl, a doctor', she repeats.

I still remember that scene well and I recall my feeling of happiness. The worries of the Maturation Exam and the University entry exam were behind me. My dream had come true. I was a first-year student at the Medical Academy in Lodz, the city we lived in at that time. A new chapter of my life had opened; I became a part of the adult world, not as a spectator, as I had been until now, but as a member with all rights and privileges, and new worries– adults' worries, as I soon found out.

During the first two years of my study, I learnt from books, lectures and tutorials about the human body and diseases, looking forward with great anticipation and excitement to the beginning of the third year, the year that marked the clinical part of my training. From then on we would deal with real patients. It was Mr Kowalski who had a heart attack, and Mrs Wrobel, who suffered from acute appendicitis and had to be operated on immediately. Those people were ill, and illnesses disrupted their lives, affecting their families. My dream about bringing help to sick people had limitations. Some patients couldn't be cured; they would die. It was real life in its concentrated form, intensified, and I was like a sponge soaking up those experiences and emotions.

Ten years after the end of the war we still had a shortage of proper teaching facilities, and our gynaecology lectures were in the old cinema built before the Second World War. Above the main entrance to the slate-grey building in gold metal letters was the word ATHENAEUM. Inside the theatre hung the musty smell of an old room without windows and fresh air. The crystal chandeliers, trimmed in gold leaf, spread dimmed light over the dark wood of the chairs, the red carpet, and the heavy red plush curtain.

It was the place where I had watched Greta Garbo and Gary Cooper, but that Thursday morning in April 1954 I sat there in the first box with my notebook on my lap ready for the words of Professor Rydel, my gynaecology lecturer.

He was an old-style real gentleman. In a grey suit, a bow tie and with his silver hair he looked like an actor playing the role of a good, gentle father. All the female students, and there were over fifty percent of us that year, liked him very much.

During the lecture he had a habit of walking along the edge of the stage, watching us. There was something warm but also penetrating in the gaze of his green eyes and when he looked at me, I always thought that he could see not only what was in my head, but also what was in my heart.

When he walked to the stage that morning and placed his papers on a little table close to the edge, he said, 'Today, we are going to talk about abortion.'

A short-lived murmur spread through the room. Zosia sitting next to me leaned forward, as if she wanted to be sure to hear the professor's every word on this special subject, a subject that in this Catholic country was still 'taboo', and not talked about in ordinary conversation, particularly in the presence of a young girl.

At that time in Poland abortion was illegal and there was a heavy jail punishment for the doctor and the woman involved. The newspapers always gave the full report of such news. I read them with the feeling that I was touching the 'dark side' of human life.

'The word "abortion" still has that dirty connotation to it'. The professor's voice was clear and strong when he continued, 'You think prostitutes are the only women who would have an abortion. You are wrong. Those women who have it are in a desperate situation; they are ordinary women, your mothers, sisters, and your friends. Often, they are victims of rape. Looking for help, they end up in the hands of unqualified, unscrupulous, and greedy people who make them ill or kill them. You'll see those women in my ward, the victims of a back-yard abortion. They are dying from sepsis, kidney diseases and poison cooked in a home-made brew.'

The lecture went on, the professor telling us about the causes of spontaneous abortion, its stages, proper diagnosis, and the treatment, explaining the surgical procedure and its possible complications. But my thoughts wandered far away from the lecture theatre.

*　*　*

I was back at the ranger's house in the forest, the place where only a few months earlier I had spent the holidays with my parents. The owners were a couple in their thirties with two children at school. He was a war invalid with one arm. She did most of the work around the place.

I remembered that one night. It was around eleven and we were ready to go to bed when there was a knock on the door of our room. My Dad opened the door. We saw our host standing in the corridor, his face pale; he was wiping tears with his one hand.

'Sorry', he said to my Dad, 'but I know you are a doctor. My wife,' he was sobbing now, 'my wife, she is bleeding, please help us, she can hardly speak, please.'

'Wait a moment,' Dad said. He grabbed his glasses and the stethoscope, and they were both gone.

My mother and I didn't sleep. The night grew darker behind the windows, and then the narrow sickle of a moon appeared in one panel of black glass and moved slowly to the next. The branch of the silver spruce growing near the window swayed in the light breeze.

'Poor woman,' my mother said. 'I hope they can get her to the hospital in time.'

Finally, in the silence of the forest's night came the distant sound of a siren. It grew louder, coming into the room, filling it with its scream, and it stopped.

'Thank God, they are here,' my mother said. 'I hope it's not too late for her.'

We both listened to the noises coming from outside the house. People talked and there was the metallic scraping sound of the stretcher being pulled out of the ambulance, the crunch of the gravel when they wheeled it alongside the path, and the sound of rushing footsteps. Then everything went silent again.

After some time, my mother got up and started to pace the room.

'What are they doing there? Why don't they take her immediately?' she asked.

'They must be giving her an injection to try to stop the bleeding and they need to put in an intravenous drip to give her some fluids,' I said.

At that moment we heard footsteps inside the house, and somebody spoke, 'Slowly, there is a step here, careful, now.'

There was the noise of the front door opening and again the crunch of the gravel outside. The metal slots scraped again when they pushed the stretcher in, then we heard the thump of the ambulance door shut, and the voice of my

Dad, 'Please, phone me…' The rest of his words drowned in the wailing sound of the siren that faded quickly away.

A few minutes later, Dad came to the room. He walked to the chair at the table but didn't sit down. He stood there with both hands on the back of the chair and looked at us. 'I hope she will last until they give her blood. She may need to be operated on straight away,' he said.

His gaze slid from our faces and turned to the window as if he was still seeing there the woman's face.

'I suspect someone tried to induce the abortion and made a hole in the uterus. I'm going to bed, I'm tired,' he said.

When he turned away from the table, I heard the words 'Bastards, murderers.' Dad rarely swore, he must have been really angry. And I didn't know whom he meant, the people who did it to the woman, or the lawmakers who made an abortion a criminal offence.

*　*　*

'That's all for today,' the voice of professor Rydel brought me back to the ATHENAEUM theatre and the lecture. 'I hope you already know your roster for the week of in-house training in the country hospitals. The first round will start next month. Do your homework and remember you will be dealing there with those desperate women. Don't throw a stone at them. Care for them. If nothing else, that at least is your duty as future doctors.'

Six weeks passed and at the end of May it was my turn to go to the country hospital. It was the same hospital to which the ambulance took the woman from the house where we spent those eventful last holidays.

It was a district hospital for the 100,000 people living in the town but it also had to care for the number of villages around it. It was a poor district with small farms and textile factories situated on the outskirts of the town.

There were four of us students, all girls. We stayed in the hospital for seven days and nights. We weren't allowed to leave the hospital premises and we had to be available and ready to work during the whole of our stay there.

On our first day, at a quarter to eight, we marched into the staff room at the gynecology ward. There was no one there. The room had bare white walls and sparse furniture. There was a couch, a few chairs, a desk and under the window stood a long table. On the desk, there was a stack of printed papers and open patient records. Pushed to one side was the phone. Above the desk hung a few shelves filled with textbooks. The metal filing cabinet and a chest of drawers occupied one corner of the room, in the other stood a pot-plant with a few stripe yellow-green stems of *Sansevieria trifasciata*, a plant with a nick-name of 'Mother-in-law's tongue'.

Suddenly I felt very lonely and frightened. There was nothing there around me to tell me I would be all right. It was me and the 'unknown'.

At that moment the door opened and a short woman in her forties with a thick crop of dark hair walked in, or rather rushed in, to the room. She stopped at the table, turned towards us and looked at us as a general might look at his soldiers during inspection.

'I'm Dr Sikora, a head of obs and gynae here, and I'll be your boss for this week. Welcome to the country, girls,' she said and pulled the chair to the table. She sat down and after giving us another searching look, she smiled a broad smile like a mother when she is happy with the look of her children. That motherly smile lifted my spirit. Everything will be okay, I told myself.

'Sit down,' she said. 'You need to know a few things about the type of work we do here. We don't have the newest facilities and large staff like the teaching hospitals in the big cities. But we have plenty of work, very often more than we can cope with, but we have to, and we do. If you work hard, do your duty, there won't be any problems –'

She was talking and I watched her, thinking that I already liked this woman. She must love her job; I could feel it. And I thought that she must be tough, hard as a rock and maybe even rough, but that was what I needed. Somebody solid as a rock, somebody I could trust and I wouldn't be afraid to ask for advice. Somebody who would be ready to teach me, not theory but the practical things, which I would need later in everyday medical life, when I would be alone to deal with whatever came to me.

'In a few minutes you will meet the rest of our staff. Doctor Pinska is responsible for you during your stay here and you will go to her if you have any house-keeping problems.' The boss paused and then pointing to the notice board hanging above the chest of drawers she said, 'Pinned to the board is a roster for your turns in the operating theatre and delivery room, and you know that you will be called to any emergency after your usual hours of work.'

In the following two days we were trying to find our place in the routine work of very busy wards and to be helpful, as much as we were able to, without interrupting the work of overtired doctors. They were friendly and made a special effort to teach as much as they could.

In the teaching hospital during our classes, we had been mostly observers. Here I was thrilled when for the first time in my student life, under supervision of the boss, I was allowed to stitch the incision made during the delivery. I also did the internal examination in women suspected of uterine and ovarian cancer and assisted during a hysterectomy. In the last case I was only standing at the table holding the retractors but washing up for this operation in that special ritualistic way, and being dressed like a real surgeon, was enough to keep me excited for the rest of that day.

On the third evening we were just finishing our meal when through an open window came the sound of a siren. First faint, it was getting louder and louder. Ambulance? Fire brigade? We looked at each other listening. Was it going to pass us, or would it stop here? The siren died abruptly; silence filled the room.

That night Zosia and I were on the roster for the admission room. We rushed downstairs.

When we arrived, Dr Kobiela, our doctor on duty was already there squatting next to the stretcher that stood in the middle of the room. On the stretcher lay a woman. Her face was as white as the sheet covering her slim, short body, eyes closed, sunken, the oxygen mask covering her nose and mouth.

The ambulance doctor, not much older than us, visibly nervous, was referring the patient to Dr Kobiela who now busy with the examination of the woman, and simultaneously giving orders to the nurse for the intravenous drip and urgent blood tests for the red cell count, blood group and blood crossing.

The tension filling the room overwhelmed me. I had to control the shaking of my hands when I helped the nurse with the intravenous drip. At the same time, I tried to listen to the short, broken sentences of the ambulance doctor's report.

'...Vaginal bleeding...thirty-two years...lives in the country...small farm...pregnancy over three months...she said, she was chopping the wood and started to bleed... deteriorated on the way... bled more on the way.'

The intravenous drip was in and blood taken for the test. Zosia got the order to phone the operating theatre to be ready immediately.

Dr Kobiela turned his head towards Zosia and me and said in a quiet voice, 'It looks as if it could be a perforated uterus.'

'I asked her if she had tried to do something,' the ambulance doctor was talking again, 'but here we always get the same answers, "chopping wood", "carrying sacks of potatoes" or "a cow kicked them in the stomach".'

The tiredness and tone of resignation were audible in his voice. From the corner of my eye, I watched him when with great relief he sat at the desk and started to fill in some forms.

Dr Kobiela bent over the patient and holding the woman's hand said slowly, 'We will give you some blood, some injections and then we will examine you in the theatre. After that we could be able to tell you more, but it seems that you may need an operation to stop this bleeding.'

The woman opened her eyes and whispered, 'Thank you.'

'Do you have children?' asked Dr Kobiela.

'Two. Seven and five years old,' answered the ambulance doctor.

'Nurse,' Dr Kobiela stood up and turned towards the admission room nurse. 'We will shift the patient to our trolley, and she needs to be taken straight to the theatre. I'll be there in a few minutes.'

Before the trolley with the woman left the room the ambulance driver came in and exchanged a few words with his doctor. The doctor collected his papers.

'I have to go,' he said. 'There is an unconscious drunk, badly bashed, at the railway station. Goodbye.' He grinned and added, 'for now'.

The driver took the stretcher and they both hurried out of the room.

I looked at Dr Kobiela. He talked on the phone. He put down the receiver and turning to Zosia and me said, 'The boss will be here soon. And you girls run to the theatre and wash up. You will assist us.'

The woman survived the operation of stitching the hole in the uterus. According to Dr Sikora the perforation was probably a result of a manipulation with a metal knitting needle, the most common 'instrument' used by unqualified person trying to induce an abortion.

The day before the woman's discharge Dr Sikora called me to her office. I received the task of giving the patient a 'special talk' about prevention of pregnancy.

'...calendar, condom and the rest, all that you know on that subject,' the boss said to me. 'But the most important thing is,' Dr Sikora added with a special emphasis, 'You have to explain to that woman that if something like this happens again, she won't survive it– for sure.'

The next morning, I ushered the patient into a small examination room. She was already dressed in her own clothes, threadbare, faded from the sun and constant washing.

We sat at the desk facing each other. She kept her hands on the top of the desk, clasped as for prayer. The rough skin of her hands was marked with scratches, scars, and calluses. Those hands told me more about her hard work and her life than any notes.

I looked at her face, still pale, and I felt sorry for her. I wanted to help her, so with all my enthusiasm I delivered my 'lecture'.

The woman listened patiently. Her face didn't show any emotion. At the end of my talk, I repeated to her Doctor Sikora's words, and then I asked the woman if she understood everything I had said and if she had any questions.

The woman looked straight at me, with her sunken blue eyes in black circles. Her pale lips trembled when she said that she understood everything, she didn't want more children, they hardly had enough food for them now, and that she knew about counting days and the condom. While she spoke two big tears were making their way down in the grooves of her cheeks. She didn't move, only clasped her hand tighter.

I was silent.

Then in a weak but even voice, as if she were talking about ordinary facts of her life she said, 'My husband…I told him many times, I can't…I don't want to sleep with him on those nights. You should see my husband, doctor. He is twice as big as me…He is not a bad man, but he drinks. And when he is drunk, he rapes me.'

There was no answer to the woman's problem in my medical textbooks.

*   *   *

Three days later, the four of us said thank you to Dr Sikora and her staff and we left that hospital to go back to our city and our previous lives.

At home, when I was telling my parents about that week in the country hospital, I realized that my week there not only gave me a taste of the real life as a future doctor, but it also changed me and some of my views forever.

The Newborn

It was June 1954. White-pink blossoms covered the chestnut trees in the parks of Lodz. The fragrance of acacias and lilac lingered in the warm air, but I had no time to enjoy it. My fourth-year final exams were coming in a rush. Every few days I went through the same cycle, first fear and panic, then short lasting relief and then my anxiety grew again rapidly as the time sped towards the next test.

My parents tried to calm me down by talking at the dinner table about everything else except my exams, but I was usually 'deaf' during those conversations. My thoughts circled around the subject I studied during the day.

That Tuesday evening Dad was late from his hospital. I was hungry and Mum was angry because the meal was going to be 'spoiled'.

Finally, the key turned in the front door and Dad came in. On his face, instead of its usual serious expression, he had a big smile that lifted the corners of his mouth and made him look like a boy happy with the world.

After giving Dad a brief kiss and a few crisp words about his late coming, Mum disappeared into the kitchen to serve the dinner. I was sure she hadn't noticed Dad's smile.

I took his small doctor's bag. 'I'll carry it to your desk,' I said.

I liked the smell of that bag, the 'doctor's smell'. The bag made of thick leather contained Dad's stethoscope, two different sized stainless-steel containers with sterile syringes and needles kept in ethanol, a pack of sterile gauze swabs and a small bottle of ethanol. There were also a few ampoules of different emergency drugs and a prescription pad. He always kept his Waterman fountain pen Dad always kept in the pocket of his jacket.

When we finally sat at the table Dad didn't start eating but holding his spoon said, 'You are not going to believe it when I tell you what happened today in the hospital.'

'You'd better eat the soup first before it gets cold,' my mother said but Dad seemed not to hear her and continued.

'A few minutes after I arrived at my ward, I heard the siren. Through one of my windows, I saw the Fire Brigade truck coming towards the hospital gate. Then the siren stopped. I wasn't sure what was going on at if the fire was somewhere within the hospital, so I looked out through the other window that faces the emergency entrance. The Fire Brigade truck was just parked in the ambulance bay. Then a fireman got out of the truck and rushed towards Casualty. He carried in both hands a small bundle wrapped in a grey blanket.

'And then I had a phone call. It was the nurse from Casualty. She was asking me to come down and examine the newborn brought in by the Fire Brigade. She thought it must have been born a short time ago as his umbilical cord wasn't even tied properly.'

'I rushed down. In the Casualty doorway I met our admitting doctor, Dr Miller. Without a word we walked in, and straight to the examining table on which lay the newborn. Two nurses were busy washing it. The infant tried to cry, just a few notes that sounded like a kitten's. And there was a terrible smell in the room, a smell of sewerage' –

'Oh no, not while we're eating,' Mum protested.

'Mum please, let Dad talk,' I said.

Dad grinned at Mum, 'Sorry Lilka, as I said, the whole admission room smelled like a sewer. One of the nurses must have noticed the expression on my face because she said, "They found him in the toilet, poor lad." I heard her but I was already busy examining the infant and I didn't ask then about the details of his rescue.'

'Is he all right? The infant?' Mum asked.

'He is well-developed and in perfect health, a beautiful boy. Must be at full term and delivered a short time before he was found. When I finished checking him, the nurse wrapped him in fresh nappies and then the baby boy gave his first real cry. He was obviously hungry. The nurses rushed out to prepare a bottle for him and Dr Miller phoned our pediatric ward to organize the boy's admission. We need to keep him under observation in the hospital for at least for two, three weeks.' Dad's voice became serious, and he didn't smile when he added, 'I hope he hasn't caught anything nasty from the excrement.'

'Lucky he was discovered alive,' Mum said, 'but how was the Fire Brigade involved in all of that?'

'The fireman who brought in the infant told us the whole story.' Dad finished eating and while he was filling his pipe with tobacco he continued talking, 'You know that waiting area at the last loop of the city trams near the hospital,' he said. 'There is a toilet building. It stands separately just on the edge of Bieganski Park.'

'That toilet is horrible. The stench inside is enough to make you vomit,' I said. 'How do you know?' Mum looked at me puzzled.

I turned towards Mum. 'You forget I had my clinical part of infectious diseases at Dad's hospital. I know that tram loop well,' I said. 'And the toilet – only once I tried to use it, but I just couldn't, and I had to run straight to the hospital and Dad's ward instead.' I shook my head. 'That toilet is worse than any outdoor country loo. It has poor lighting and is littered with rubbish. The wooden benches in the cubicles have cut holes and there are no covers for them. The septic tank must be under it,' I hesitated and shivered recalling the picture and then I said, 'It was warm weather when I was there, and all I could see through the hole was a dense mass of excrement, crawling with maggots and blow flies on top.'

'This is really awful.' Mum screwed her face in disgust. 'And that infant was there? It's a wonder he didn't drown.'

'Luckily for him there must be a thick mass in that tank. Maybe the tank leaks.' Dad said. 'Anyway, the fireman told us that they received the emergency call from one of the tram drivers who went to the toilet and then heard a noise from down below. He looked through the hole and saw that there was a baby. He called his conductor and another driver for help, but when they realized there was no way they could reach that baby they called the Fire Brigade. The fireman lifted the infant out and took it to the nearest hospital, which was ours.'

'And the mother? Do you know anything about her?' Mum asked.

'No. Not really. The police were notified straight away, and they are doing their usual enquiry. They came to the hospital at midday and told us they thought it could be one of the young girls working as conductors. She probably delivered that boy somewhere in that nearby park in the early hours of the morning and then threw him into the toilet.'

'Poor girl. She must have been in shock and desperate to do something like that,' Mum said and for some time we sat there in silence.

We finished our tea. Mum got up and started to collect the dirty dishes on a tray. Before she took it to the kitchen, she turned to Dad saying, 'You need to tell us how the boy progresses over the next few days. I hope that it will be another miracle, and he stays healthy', Mum said.

In the following weeks we received from Dad a daily bulletin about the boy. It must have been another 'miracle', as Mum had said earlier, but the boy, according to Dad, 'didn't even sneeze' and was developing well.

His story and his daily progress travelled fast on the hospital grapevine and there were constant visitors to the pediatric ward to have a look at the boy.

One day, Dad told us that the police had found the mother. As they had suspected it was a tram conductor, a seventeen-year-old girl. She was charged with the offence, and Dad said that the child would soon be officially ready for adoption.

'It is really unbelievable,' Dad said, how many people among the hospital staff want to adopt this boy. Yesterday, the nurse in my ward, she's married, but I know they don't have children, told me she put her name on the list. She firmly believed that boy's survival was a real miracle and that he will not only have a great future, but he will also bring good luck to his adoptive parents.'

'Good luck to all of them,' Mum said. 'The boy deserves it, and I hope he will be loved by his family.' She hesitated and looked at me. 'I still think about that poor girl, his mother, and I wonder if she ever gives him a thought…maybe that will come later to her… the regret…he is her son.'

It's a Boy

They rooted out of me
three kilograms of flesh, bones, blood
a ball of grey cells and white fibres wrapped in slippery
skin
a wrinkled fig dipped in wax

An arrow shoots from a circle
it's a boy

Who is he going to be?

Einstein regretting his atomic research, a screen idol
playing everyman's wars, or a patriotic hero resurrected
on a monument in a foreign country

today he is only my son

People

During my medical studies and in my professional work I looked at all my patients in the same way, regardless of gender. Never did my male patients raise in my mind any 'undercurrent' of thoughts, except for reminding me about the differences in our anatomy and behaviour, and the need of addressing them professionally.

As a female medical student, and later a woman doctor, dealing with patients of the opposite sex, sometimes placed me in awkward, or funny situations. Those encounters tested not only my knowledge and my medical skills, but they also widened my life experience.

* * *

Dr Skalski, the surgical registrar, checked his watch. After a quick glance over our small group of fifth year students he said, 'Ten to eight and you are all here. That's very good. Punctuality is so important.'

He didn't smile and we stood there without a word, waiting. We had already learned during our previous week at that ward that Dr Skalski rarely smiled. We also learned that he was a very demanding teacher.

After he ticked off our names on his list he said, 'I have very interesting patients for you today. Basia,' he turned to me, 'we'll start with you.' He looked at his notes. 'You'll have Mr. Bogusz– admitted last night. He had an accident and needed a few stitches on his scrotum. You can't see the wound; we'll talk about it later. He is on the stretcher in the corridor.'

After assigning other patients to my six colleagues, Dr Skalski closed his notes and before he hurried out, he said, 'I'll meet with all of you in half an hour in the corridor in front of the staff room.'

We hastened to our tasks.

Several stretchers were parked along the wall of a long corridor, a sign that the night was 'heavy' with work and emergency admissions. I found my patient on the third stretcher. The man in his thirties had a mop of dark hair. His face with a day's growth looked pale and distressed. His eyes were shut. When I introduced myself, he opened his eyes, blinked, and grimaced as if in pain but he didn't speak.

'Do you have any pain now?' I asked.

'I got an injection...it still hurts a lot,' the man said quietly without looking at me.

I checked the patient's card hanging on the side of his stretcher. 'You'll get more of the painkiller soon,' I said. 'I'm sorry but I need to ask you about your accident.'

The man nodded. I noticed his hands. They were labourer's hands with hardened, thick skin, calluses, and old scars. Grey lines of dirt outlined his chipped nails.

'Was it at work, this accident?' I asked lowering my voice. The next stretcher was parked less than two metres away.

'No. At home,' he said.

'What were you doing?'

The man looked at me but then he turned his gaze to the wall.

'I was picking apples... branch broke... I fell from the ladder... cut myself down there'– he pointed to his crotch– 'on a branch.' He spoke slowly– guarding his words.

It was strange, I thought, watching the man in front of me. There was not a scratch or a bruise on the man's face or neck, nor on his uncovered forearms.

'Did you injure yourself anywhere else during your fall?'

'No,' he said firmly. Then he hesitated and added, 'but the pain was terrible. It made me feel dizzy and nauseous. I was bleeding a lot. My wife called the ambulance,' he said.

My physical examination of the patient didn't add anything new. His scrotum was covered by the dressing and there were no scratches or bruises on the rest of his body.

*　*　*

'We have six patients to see,' the registrar said to our small group assembled at the door of the staff room. He checked his notes and turned to me. 'You had Mr Bogusz. We'll start with him, but first you tell us what you learned from the patient?'

'Not much,' I said and repeated the story I'd heard from Mr. Bogusz. 'He was very vague in his answers,' I added.

'I'm not surprised,' the registrar grinned. 'And on examination, anything special?'

'I couldn't find any signs of other injuries, not even a scratch on his skin,' I said.

Something like a smile flickered over Dr Skalski's face before he said, 'We all know and you were told many times, that taking a good history from the patient is a very important part of the patient's examination. You also have been taught that *a patient is always right,* and you should pay great attention to his or her complaints. As always there are exceptions to the rules. Sometimes your findings during the physical examination may give you a different picture to the story the patient told you. Then you need to believe the facts in front of your eyes.'

This time Dr Skalski smiled and continued. 'We heard the story Mr Bogusz told Basia about his accident. And she said she was surprised with the lack of lacerations on his body.' The registrar stopped and looked at us. 'She didn't see the wound, but I examined it and I'm certain that the wound on Mr Bogusz's scrotum couldn't be caused by a broken branch. It is a clean, fortunately not too deep cut, as if made by a sharp instrument– a knife or a razor.'

Dr Skalski turned to me. 'In this case Mr Bogusz didn't want to tell you the truth. I reckon the patient's wound is the job of his jealous wife or lover, and it was done with a very sharp razor. It must hurt like hell, but he is lucky she didn't cut off his penis or his testis.'

He watched us for a moment. Then he frowned and in his usual serious manner said, 'Nothing new. We have seen similar cases before. You'll learn. People...' he shook his head. Then he checked his watch. 'We'd better have a look at Mr Bogusz's wound. After him we will see Zosia's patient, Mrs Korona.'

Good Care

At ten to eight we were all in the staff room ready for the morning meeting. Dr Werner drank the last of his coffee and stretched his shoulders. The signs of a sleepless night were visible on his face. During the previous twenty-four hours, he and Dr Bilski had been on duty while the ward was covering the emergency admissions of surgical patients from the area of the town designated to us.

At five to eight Dr Adamiec, head of the ward, entered the staff room. He greeted us with 'Good morning' and took his usual place at the top of the table.

'We'd better start,' he said and pointing to the stack of patients' records in front of Dr Werner he added, 'You must have been busy.'

'Yes. We operated all night.' Dr Werner said. He looked at the folder in his hand and started his report – 'Mr Kowal, a young man...acute appendicitis, we operated on him straight away. He is doing fine.' Dr Werner reached for another patient's record, 'Mr Waluk, forty-nine, admitted at one a.m. drunk, stab wound to the thigh, complicated... I had to repair...'

Fascinated, I sat amongst my older colleagues trying not to miss a word from the report and following discussions full of Latin terms and surgeons' specific jargon.

It was the sixth year of my studies, the year of practical hospital training in the four major specialities – internal diseases, surgery, obstetrics and gynaecology, and paediatrics. I wanted to do real work during that training, not just observe, as I did in the teaching hospitals. For my surgery I had specifically applied for this ward, in the district public hospital.

The ward had a small team of skilled surgeons and a good reputation in medical circles. And now after four weeks of work I felt like a very small, but real part of it. I was directly supervised by two men, Dr. Bilski and Dr Werner. Dr Bilski, with light, receding hair, and pale skin, was jovial, short and stocky. Dr Werner had dark hair, olive skin and he was tall and bony, with a long face and arms. Dr Bilski talked a lot, especially during the long hours at the operating table, while Dr Werner was a man of a very few words. I liked them both.

They were busy but they always found time to teach me. Under their supervision I was already allowed to do minor surgical procedures such as stitching wounds and open and drain abscesses. During twenty-four-hour emergency duties, often at night, I assisted in major operations. This, I thought, was at the very doorway to medical heaven.

*　*　*

After one of the morning meetings Dr Bilski gave me a patient's folder saying, 'Mr Michalak was admitted early this morning. He is in room 4. He is yours.'

I waited for the surgeon's usual mischievous smile and maybe a joke, but nothing came. His face looked indifferent. He was already at the door when he turned towards me and said, 'Take good care of this patient. He has a serious problem.' This time, I thought, there was a twinkle in Dr Bilski's eye.

From the patient's records I learnt that Mr Michalak was two years older than me, a PhD student in Acoustic Engineering at the Politechnik. He had severe inflammation of the testicle and there was suspicion of underlying malignancy. Dr Bilski was right; the man had a serious problem. If not treated properly, the inflammation could cause infertility, and a malignant tumour of the testis if confirmed was a terrible diagnosis.

I took the patient records and walked to room 4. There were twelve men there and only one looked the age of my new patient.

Next to him was another of my patients, forty-two-year-old Mr Lech, with cancer of the stomach. He had been operated on a few days previously, but it had been too late for him, the tumour was already inoperable.

I checked Mr Michalak's name against the page of treatment chart hanging on the end of the bed, said, 'Good morning', and I introduced myself.

'Good morning, Doctor.' The patient answered my greeting in a barely audible voice. He pulled the blanket up to his shoulders and lay on his back as stiff as a mummy. In a round face, his cheeks were flushed due to a high temperature. He had blond hair with a fringe that he tried to sweep away from his forehead, but it fell back, and he gave up, keeping both hands under the blanket. He watched me intensely with his grey eyes. He was visibly nervous.

'I need to ask you a few questions and later I need to examine you,' I said in my most professional voice. I smiled a little trying to make him feel more comfortable. For me he was just another patient, and interesting too, because I had never seen a case like this before. But he seemed embarrassed by my presence or perhaps, my gender.

His answers to my questions were short and I had to really drag them from him. He surrendered without a word to my examination. When I asked him to pull down his pyjama pants, he did it with hesitation and turned his head away towards the window.

His left testicle was swollen, the scrotum over it was red and hot. It must have been very painful for him.

I finished the examination and told him he could dress again. When I was making a few notes in my notebook, he said, 'Doctor, excuse me...'

I looked at him, 'Yes?' I said.

'Is it really bad? My disease?' he asked in a small trembling voice.

And then I realised that he was not so much embarrassed by a young female doctor examining him, as he was frightened of his disease. This was his first serious health problem, and he was intelligent enough to realise the consequences.

I felt sorry for him. I smiled. 'Don't worry,' I said. 'You're having antibiotics; they should work soon. I'm sure in two to three days you will feel a lot better. You will need to have blood and urine tests today and tomorrow as well.'

'Thank you, Doctor,' he said with a weak smile. His body, so tense before, seemed to relax under the hospital blanket.

When I came back to the staff room everybody was already there having a cup of coffee. I put the patient's records on the small desk where I usually worked, took a cup and started to make myself a coffee.

'Here is our Basia, future star of surgery,' Dr Bilski said loudly behind my back. 'Have you seen your patient yet?'

'Yes', I said. With my cup already full I turned to face the room and my colleagues, five men and one woman. They all smiled. Only Dr Werner's long face had its usual serious expression. I was sure they all knew from Dr Bilski about my patient, and they now waited for my reaction. I tried hard not to blush, but blushing has always been my curse, and the hot wave spread from my neck and face to the edge of my hair.

Dr Bilski's smile widened. 'Sit down here, before you spill that coffee.' He made a space for me next to him on the small couch. 'We have a few minutes now to talk about your patient,' he said.

I sat down. To steady my hands, I held my cup of coffee firmly while I reported to my audience the findings about Mr Michalak.

'Very good,' Dr Bilski said, and he asked me a few questions about the management of such cases, probable outcome, and further prognosis. Then they all discussed my patient in detail.

Soon that short meeting was over, and everyone hurried out of the room. I was walking with Dr Bilski to the admission room to see a new patient. On the way he talked about the operations rostered for the next day and then he touched my arm and said, 'You did a good job with your patient.'

It sounded like real praise. I looked at him. His face was serious but then he grinned, and there were sparks of laughter in his eyes when he said, 'It is important that in the following days you keep a detailed record of the patient's progress, of his complaints and the changes in physical examination.' With those words he pushed open the door to the admission room.

In the next week life in the ward took its usual course, filled with hours spent at the operating tables and dressing room, and a hectic time in the admission room during emergency duties. On top of that were daily ward rounds, staff meetings and plenty of boring paperwork.

As I was instructed, I saw Mr Michalak every day, examined him and wrote notes in his record. The antibiotics did the job, he was improving. He was still nervous and tense, and hesitant in answering my routine questions.

One morning, during our ward round, Dr Bilski examined my patient and said, 'You are doing very well Mr Michalak'. Dr Bilski smiled. 'Keep going like that and you will be ready to go home soon.'

'Thank you, Doctor. I feel better. It is not hurting so much now,' the patient said but didn't smile. He lay without movement clutching the blanket to his chest. His anxious gaze fixed on Dr Bilski who was looking through the patient's records.

'That's good,' Dr Bilski said giving me the folder. He turned back to the patient and with a big grin he added, 'Nothing to worry about. Your family jewels are in perfect order.'

This time a big smile and a blush spread over the patient's round face.

The next day when I came to see him, he was sitting in bed reading a book. 'I can study now,' he said, putting the book away. 'I have an exam coming soon, but I couldn't look at those books. I was so frightened, couldn't stop thinking that it was cancer.' He lowered his voice, nodding towards Mr Lech in the next bed, and when he looked back at me, the old anxiety was back in his eyes. 'If it had been cancer, nothing would have been important anymore. I couldn't sleep'–

'You can forget it now. Dr Bilski told you all is well.'

'I know. Thank you. I'm so relieved. But...' he hesitated, looked around the room and then at me and said, 'I don't know Doctor, how you can deal with all that. I could never be a doctor.'

In the following days Dr Bilski remarked a few times about my patient and 'my good care of him' that must have helped his recovery. But to Dr Bilski's disappointment I didn't rise to the bait.

On the day of Mr Michalak's discharge I prepared his documents and went to him. He was still in his pyjamas, but his clothes lay on the bed. He was packing his books into a small backpack. He smiled when he saw me.

'Good morning', I said smiling back. 'Here is your Information Card, with a summary of your stay in the Hospital to show to your doctor, and a referral to the urologist for a check-up.' I gave him both papers and held my hand out to him, 'Goodbye,' I said. 'And good luck with your exam,' I added.

He stood up, took the piece of paper, and shook my hand. 'Thank you, thank you very much, Doctor,' he said.

I turned and was on my way out when he asked, 'Oh Doctor, you will be in the ward around midday?'

'Yes,' I said a bit puzzled, and I left the room.

* * *

Around midday all of us, except Dr Bilski, were in the staff room ready for the meeting that was about to start. Br Bilski came in and said loudly, 'Basia, your patient Mr. Michalak is waiting for you in the corridor.'

'I gave him all the discharge papers early this morning,' I said.

'But he's asked for you specially. You'd better go,' Dr Bilski grinned watching me blushing this time.

I went out. A few metres from the door I saw my patient with a huge bouquet of yellow and red tulips. He rushed towards me.

I stood stunned.

'I wanted specially to thank you, Doctor,' he said giving me the flowers.

'It's very nice of you but really it wasn't necessary,' I said thinking that it must have cost him a lot of money, and as a student he probably didn't have much. 'Thanks again,' I said, ready to go back to the staff room.

'Excuse me Doctor,' he hesitated, 'I would like to ask you if we could meet for coffee one day?'

I gazed at him trying to find the right words to say no without hurting him. Finally, I said, 'I'm sorry, but I won't have time for that, I am really very busy. Goodbye.'

I hurried into the staff room. My colleagues looked at me and the flowers and there was a loud '*Ohhhhh*'...

'Your care must have' – Dr Bilski started in loud whisper, but Dr Werner interrupted him, 'Tadek, enough. Leave Basia alone.' And turning to me he said, 'The flowers are beautiful.'

Goodbye Doctor

In 1962 Poland was a country of great shortages and long queues. People stood on the street for hours to buy a loaf of bread and off-cuts of meat that was mostly bones.

At that time, I was working as a second-year registrar in a major teaching hospital. It was my teenager's dream to be a doctor. That dream had become a reality when I got my diploma, a piece of paper that opened for me the door to the real world I had been so anxious to enter, the world where patients were not cases in medical books but real people who were ill and needed my professional help.

Soon I was going to learn that for some of those patients it wasn't enough to be cured of their disease. They needed other help which neither I, nor anybody else in Poland at that time, could provide for them.

On that cold November morning in the crowded tram, I thought with excitement about my work, making in my mind a list of things that I needed to do during the day. The list was long: patients, students, reports, staff meeting, papers for a conference, not counting any emergency events.

'Good morning.' I greeted the guard at the Hospital gate and walked the path through the garden towards the main entrance. To open the door carved in black oak, I had to push it with my shoulder. A few steps and I was in the main entrance hall from where a marble staircase led to the second and third floors. The winter sun, coming through the six-metre-tall leadlight windows, filled the well of the hall with light and drew a colourful mosaic on the white marble floor. The beauty of that place struck me always as a reminder of the past, "the better times" my parents so often talked about.

My ward was in front of me. The smell of illness mixed with disinfectant and cooked food were all familiar. It was my place.

'Hi Witek,' I said to the resident working with me that year. 'I see you had a busy night. How many stretchers are there?'

Witek was a short, plump man, always smiling. The patients liked him. He looked at the stretchers lined along the wall of the long corridor and said, 'There were twenty admissions over the night. I had to borrow beds from surgical; we ran out of ours.'

'I'll be ready in a few minutes,' I said and walked to the staff room to get my white coat. I locked my handbag away and, putting the stethoscope in my pocket, I thought it was nothing new for us not to have enough beds. There was a shortage of everything – houses, food, clothes, medicines – but no shortage of patients. The war and six years of German occupation had left its mark. There was no Marshall Plan aid money for Poland.

'First we'll see our men,' I said to Witek. When we opened the door of one of the biggest rooms, the smell of vomit hit my nostrils, forcing me to hold my breath. It took me a few moments to regain control. 'Good morning, gentlemen!' I said in a loud voice.

'Good morning, Doctor.' It sounded like a choir that needed a lot of practice.

Twenty beds separated by night tables were crammed into the room. No curtains. Life, with all its most intimate functions, was uncovered for everyone's eyes. Only the bed in the far corner of the room had a portable screen. Behind that screen was a patient dying from the end stage of carcinoma of the pancreas. We wanted to move him to a smaller room but both small rooms were full. No luxury of privacy, even for the dying. Just the screen. The screen and the dead man would later be removed together. We were used to that. Nothing else could be done.

After seeing the first three patients who had been admitted during the night, we moved to bed number four. The shape under the thin hospital blanket resembled a twiggy teenager, but the head was of an old man. Sharp features, white bushy hair and a beard gave the man a biblical appearance.

'Mr Kubacki was brought by ambulance from the nursing home,' Witek spoke looking through his notes. 'He has pneumonia. It must have been going on for some time.'

The man didn't move. His hands lay flat on the blanket. They looked like pieces of rough wood with nodes sticking out. An intravenous drip was attached to his left forearm. Through his wrinkled skin I could see the network of veins. The man's hand, when I took it to feel for his pulse, was like part of a skeleton, all bones, no muscles, no fat. The hand felt hot. The man was silent, but he watched me, alert to my every move. 'We need to do something about your temperature, Mr Kubacki,' I said. 'Please sit up. I'd like to listen to your chest.'

When I unbuttoned the jacket of his hospital pyjamas and put my stethoscope on his protruding ribs, I had to support him with my other hand. 'You're very weak, Mr Kubacki, not much flesh on you. What about your appetite?'

It was a routine question, but I should not have asked it, not of this man; I knew he lived in a nursing home. Once, I visited my mother's friend in one of them and I still remembered the terrible conditions there. Run by the state, the nursing homes were overcrowded, dirty places, staffed with an inadequate number of carers often ready to steal food and other goods provided for the patients. My mother's friend was demented, so it didn't matter to her where she was. But for someone with the full capacity of his brain, it must be hell being in such place, I thought, looking at the man.

When we were leaving him, the patient said in a harsh voice, 'Thank you, Doctor.'

Over the next few days Mr Kubacki improved dramatically. His temperature was normal, the cough had settled down and the changes in his lungs, previously audible by auscultation, were now minimal. Witek made sure the patient had a diet with all the nutritional additions reserved for special cases.

During our visits the patient didn't talk much, just 'yes' or 'no' to my questions. He never smiled. From the moment when we left his bed, he closed his eyes, but he didn't sleep.

On the way to the staff room I said to Witek, 'I have never seen Mr Kubacki reading or talking to other people. He just lies there with his eyes closed.'

'He doesn't need a book. He has enough in his past to write one.'

'What did he do before the war?'

'He taught mathematics in a high school. He had a wife and two daughters. They lived in Warsaw, with his parents.'

There was something in Witek's voice that made me stop a few metres before the door to our usually crowded staff room. We stood at the bay window filled with leafy plants, a small oasis of living green in the white hospital environment. Behind the glass the garden looked grey and sad. The sun was gone and drops of November rain hung on the bare branches of the maple tree next to the window.

'What happened later, during the German occupation?' I asked Witek.

'His mother was not a Jew, but his father was.' Witek was looking at me, our eyes met, and then he turned his gaze towards the garden. 'They took the whole family, except him. He was lucky, at the time he was visiting his younger sister who lived with friends in another town. The family was killed in Auschwitz. The sister was helped by her Polish friends, and he joined the underground army. They both survived. After the war they lived together. When he developed tuberculosis and later heart problems his sister

83

took care of him. But she died a year ago and he had to go to a special accommodation home. He couldn't care for himself.'

In silence we both watched the rain now lashing the glass in front of us. 'We have to go,' I said and started to walk towards our staff room. On the way my thoughts were still with Mr Kubacki. His story was one of many stories typical of that time. So typical, it didn't evoke much sympathy from others. People became tired of hearing them and numb in some ways.

It was ten days after the admission of Mr Kubacki, when Professor Morski, during a ward round said to him, 'You look a different man now, Mr Kubacki. You must be feeling well. I think you are ready to go home.'

The man didn't say anything, and the Professor continued, 'It will be better for you. Here, you may only catch some other nasty thing.' Bending his long figure towards me he added, 'We need beds, Basia, please discharge Mr Kubacki soon.'

I came back to the patient later. 'You heard the Professor,' I said, 'I think you are well enough to go soon.'

'Yes, I heard the Professor,' he said, 'but please, Doctor, let me stay here longer, please. I feel so good here.'

'I can't, even if I wanted to keep you here.' To add weight to my words I said, 'The Professor was right. Staying longer in the hospital, for a man like you, there is always a danger of catching something else. It will be better for you to go home.'

After a few moments of silence, the man said, 'You don't know Doctor, what it was like in that home. I can't go back there. I would rather kill myself than go there.' 'Don't talk like that, please Mr Kubacki,' I said. 'I understand. Those places are not very good, but you know, you don't have any family, and you can't be alone. We don't have any other place to send you.'

Again, the picture of the nursing home came to my mind. I hesitated, 'Alright, we may need another x-ray of your chest and some blood tests. It will take a few more days, but next week, I will have to discharge you.'

Later, to avoid the professor's reprimand, Witek and I invented the story that Mr Kubacki had experienced sudden chest pain, and he needed additional investigation.

A week later, we started our daily ward visit at Mr Kubacki's bed. 'I'm sorry, but you have to leave today, Mr Kubacki,' I said. 'Here are the papers with the information about your health. Your doctor and the nurse in the nursing home will need them. You know you have a weak heart, and you need to take tablets every day. Witek will give you the prescription later. An ambulance will be here just after lunch.' I stretched out my hand towards him. 'Goodbye Mr Kubacki. I hope you will be well there.'

He took my hand with both his hands and said, 'Thank you, Doctor. You were very good to me.' His pale face as always didn't show any emotion. He was still holding my hand when he said, 'I'll be all right there. Goodbye Doctor.' He let go of my hand. He didn't smile. Neither did I.

He was still in his bed, when after seeing a few more patients, Witek, and I, left the room.

Twenty minutes later, while examining a patient in the next room, we heard a loud thump followed by a woman's scream. Silence spread about the room. Witek and I rushed to the door. Once in the corridor we hesitated. Then we saw it. A young trainee nurse stood in the open doorway between the corridor and the main entrance hall. She held a leaf of the door with one hand and with the other she pointed to something on the floor.

When we came closer, I could see the girl was shaking. She quietly repeated the same words: 'Oh my God… Oh my God… Here, look here. Oh, my God…' On the floor of the entrance hall lay the body of a man in hospital clothes, his white hair and beard splashed red with blood gathering in a pool on the white marble floor.

'He jumped from the third floor,' somebody was saying, 'Just as she walked into the entrance hall. Lucky, he didn't kill her as well.'

He was dead. His death had been instant. Looking at Mr Kubacki's body, I heard his voice saying, 'I will be all right there. Goodbye Doctor.'

Living Lines are Never Straight

ECG lines rise and fall
draw an abstract form
            of being.

Behind a window
the camellia bud
yesterday
a green knot of inertia
today unfurls
            into a living cup.

In your sleep
the wall of your chest
rises and falls
on the tide of breath
a blue spider of veins
crawls on your hand.

Your body surrenders
to my fingers
in your pulse
I touch
            life's rhythm.

Polanica-Zdrój

Dr Marczak, my older colleague, threw the newspaper on the coffee table. 'So, you want to know about Polanica and what to do there,' he said with his usual grin.

He was half-leaning, half-sitting in his favourite place on a couch. He believed in an old saying, 'rush slowly' and was always the last one to leave the staff room after the morning meeting unless he was called to Emergency.

He watched me for a moment, leaned further back on a cushion and said, 'There are a few nice "holes" with a good selection of cognac and brandies for a night cap, a reasonable coffee with a midday concert of popular classical music in a café at the main Sanatorium, and not many places where you can get a decent meal when you've had enough of the sanatorium canteen food, which is rather terrible.'

I smiled, imagining myself going alone to the bar in the evening for a glass of brandy. 'But seriously, please, tell me what we are expected to do there,' I said.

'All right, work-wise'– Dr Marczak paused and held out a packet of mints. 'Would you like one?'

I took a pastille. They were his recent substitute for cigarettes.

'There is not much work really,' he said. 'You need to see all the patients when they arrive, check their medication, and prescribe any of the spa treatment you consider appropriate for them. I mean – some walking, a mineral bath, or a massage. Then you need to see them half-way through their stay and finally check them before they leave for home and write their discharge summary. Of course, you need to deal with anything that can happen at any time. Apart from that, let your patients enjoy the place.' Dr Marczak's mouth moved in a crooked smile before he added, 'Sometimes they enjoy it too much. They get drunk, or "overexcited and overworked", if you understand what I mean,' he said.

'There?' I said surprised. 'I heard that all patients' rooms are shared by two or more people. No privacy at all.'

'True. But don't underestimate our patients. They are there four weeks free from their wives and their husbands, have nothing to do, and this pleasurable activity is free. I assure you; there are always some who find a way to have sex there.'

I shook my head in disbelief. 'Maybe most of it is just gossip; such places must be buzzing with it.'

Dr Marczak smiled at me. 'Oh Basia, lucky those who are still naïve,' he said. 'I don't mind if that "un-prescribed" activity helps our patients in their recovery, but sometimes it is too much of an effort for their weak hearts and then they are in trouble.'

He stood up. 'I'm sorry, I have to go to my students,' he said. But before he left, he added, 'I think it was two years ago when a patient died during the act. Dr Boska knows that story better. It happened when she was there.'

The last piece of Dr Marczak's information made me anxious. Till now I thought about my time in Polanica as half-work and half-holiday. But suddenly I realised that I would be responsible for many patients, often with multiple medical problems, and I would be alone, far away from the support of my colleagues and my bosses.

With growing apprehension during the next few weeks, I listened to the tales and advice from my older colleagues familiar with the place and its medical facilities.

I had visited Polanica only once before, as a tourist. It was a little town in Lower Silesia in Middle Sudety Mountains. The town's origin, as a Prussian and then a German village, dated back to the fifteenth century. Four centuries later Polanica became a spa resort, well known for its medicinal mineral waters. After the Second World War the town belonged to Poland and the place kept its spa tradition under the communist regime. Our teaching hospital had a convalescence home there for the patients who experience cardiac events and heart surgery.

*　*　*

Finally, November came, and I found myself in Polanica, welcomed by the director of our sanatorium, as a doctor for a month. I started work the day after my arrival and in the following three days I saw all my patients.

As my colleagues had said, there was plenty of time left for walking and reading. During the afternoon, I also started to explore places recommended by Dr Marczak. In the evenings I indulged myself by having a mineral bath in a huge marble tub in the empty hydrotherapy area in the basement.

On the fifth day, the nurse, a practical, local woman in her fifties, told me that Mr Solasz, a patient recovering from a heart attack, would like to see me again.

'Solasz–wait a minute, yes, I remember him, a nice man. He was well when I saw him. Is something wrong with his heart? I asked.

'It's not his heart. He's complaining about pain in the testicles,' she said.

Mr Solasz, a fifty-six-year-old clerk, was a mildly overweight but fit looking man. He sat comfortably in a chair at the side of my desk while I asked him the history of his pain. Finally, I said, 'Please, Mr Solasz, lie on the couch and pull your pants down.'

He did it without any hesitation.

'Where exactly is the pain now,' I asked.

'Here', he said, and he pointed to the right side of his scrotum. I looked carefully at both sides and examined the patient thoroughly. He flinched when I touched the spot he indicated, but apart from that everything seemed normal during my physical examination. I was ready to ask him to pull up his trousers when I remembered the golden rule of my General Medicine Lecturer. He had told us that if we had a patient, a man in his forties and we didn't check his prostate, we hadn't examined that man properly.

I looked back at Mr Solasz. 'It all looks fine but to be sure that we are not missing anything I need to check your prostate,' I said.

He didn't protest and I performed the rectal examination. His prostate was normal.

When he dressed and was back in his seat I said to him, 'You say you have pain but fortunately everything looks normal there and your prostate is not enlarged. I know you told me you haven't had any problems passing urine but again, to be sure that all is well, we will do urine and blood tests.'

I turned to the nurse who was in the room with me. 'We will do that test now and I will see Mr Solasz again when we get the results.'

'I hope you will feel better soon,' I said to the patient, and I left the room.

Two days later I saw Mr Solasz again. His results were normal, but he still complained about pain, that according to him, 'was a bit less than before.' I examined him again. Nothing changed, all was normal. I reassured him that there was no reason for him to worry.

The following night I was busy with a real emergency. A sixty-year-old woman with a previous heart attack developed severe chest pain and I had to send her to the local hospital.

Four days later the nurse gave me a short list of patients I wanted to check, but at the end of it I saw Mr Solasz's name. I looked at the nurse, 'Mr Solasz, why?' I asked.

'Yes, he came this morning and said that his pain is now in his left testicle and it's getting worse.' She smiled and hesitated, 'If I may say, Doctor,' she paused.

'You may, what is it?'

She looked at me for a moment as a mother would look at her young daughter, and then she said, 'Well, I think, there is nothing wrong with Mr Solasz. He just likes to come and be touched by you. That's all,' she said.

He was the last one I saw that day. I listened to his complaints but when I examined him everything was still normal. I explained patiently to the man that I couldn't find anything wrong with him. Then I said, 'I'm sorry Mr Solasz that I can't help you. I think that if the pain doesn't get better in the next three days, I will send you to the hospital for a consultation with the urologist. You may even need to stay there for some special tests, and I must warn you, they can be painful.'

I didn't see Mr Solasz again till his due visit before his discharge, at which time, he didn't have any complaints.

* * *

'How was Polanica?' Dr Marczak asked me on my return.

'Very interesting,' I said. I smiled at him. 'The patients were very good, and I even had time to try the brandies in the places you recommended.'

'No disasters?'

'Only one emergency. A woman in her sixties suffered an acute coronary. I had to send her to the hospital. She was doing fine when I left.'

Dr Marczak grinned and lifted his eyebrows.

'Oh no, there was nothing on the grapevine about her. As a matter of fact, I hadn't heard any gossip about my patients during the whole month there,' I said.

Then I remembered Mr Solasz. I was sure that after my departure that story had spread fast through the place.

On Duty

The Hospital was getting ready for the night. The lights in the patients' rooms went off. Nurses moved quietly at their stations in half-lit corridors.

On my way through the ward, I could hear patients groaning and sighing in their sleep. The pain and suffering, even of those without any hope, had to obey the ritual of day and night. Why do we force sleep upon people who have so little time left? This evening, as so many times before, this question crossed my mind, but I was too tired to think about it. Behind me were fourteen hours in the Admission Room with only a few minutes break between patients– just enough time to drink another cup of coffee.

I looked at my watch; it was almost ten. Too late now to phone home. They must be sleeping. I could picture Stefan in his bed, duvet kicked on the floor, his four-year-old body spread eagled, short hair still wet from the bath. And my mother in my room tidying things or maybe already sleeping too, exhausted after the whole day with Stefan. 'He has so much energy, I wish I had half of it,' I could hear her words.

A wave of guilt swept through me. I knew they had been waiting for my call. But every time I had started to dial the home number there was another patient, another ambulance. A few more days like this one and I would hate this hospital and hate medicine, I thought, weaving my way between stretchers that lined both sides of the corridor. A clerk could lock her desk and go home to her family, and she could forget about work, but I–, I am always between my duties and my home.

'–*All schools are closed…many factories and offices are closing down…*' the voice of a news reader came through the half-open door to the cleaners' room.

I stopped and listened.

'*Health services are stretched to the limit…delays in ambulance response…hospitals staff overworked…*' the voice of a news reader continued, '*This epidemic of flu is being compared to the nineteen eighteen epidemic that killed more people than the First World War. The most vulnerable are the old, those with other health problems, young children and …*'

I stood there hypnotised by his voice. He was talking to me, about my parents, my son, and I – I was here, trapped in the middle of that mess, taking care of others, not even having time to call and ask…

'Doctor, I was looking for you. I phoned the Admission Room, but you had already left.'

The young nurse hurried towards me from the room across the corridor. She was carrying a tray full of dirty syringes, empty bottles, and tubes for intravenous fluids. Her white uniform was stained with blood and yellow liquid. On her white cap, which had slid towards her right ear, was a narrow black ribbon, a sign that she was straight from nursing school.

'What happened?'

'Mr Król, the old man who was admitted this afternoon, he's been bleeding.'

'He has pneumonia. I remember him,' I said. I also remembered that according to the ambulance doctor the man's whole family was sick, but the old man was in the worst state.

'It was ten minutes ago; I was just giving him an intravenous injection.' The nurse spoke quickly while walking at my side. 'I was half-way through when he started to cough. He couldn't stop. It was dry at first, but at the end he coughed up fresh blood, a lot of it.' She looked at me adding, 'He was so frightened when he saw it.'

I was sure she had been frightened too. It was her first real job and at night fears are always magnified.

We were already at the open door to Room 3. The warm air in the overcrowded room smelled of disinfectant mixed with the odour of perspiring, sick bodies.

'Mr Król is in bed five, next to the window. He was lucky. It was the only bed left when he arrived,' the nurse was telling me. 'We had just enough time to change the bed linen,' she added in a quiet voice.

From where I stood, I could see the old man's chest heaving with every breath, the oxygen tube in his nostril, the intravenous drip attached to his forearm. And then, crossing the room, I recalled that only a few hours earlier in that very bed was another patient. The bed was too short for him. 'He is growing too fast,' his mother had said.

When I looked at the empty chair beside the bed, I saw her face and I could hear her voice pleading, 'Doctor, do something, please. He is only nineteen. He is our only child. Please!' She had been sitting there, holding his hand to the end. She had not cried. According to my medical book, the boy had rapidly progressing haemorrhagic pneumonia due to a flu virus. That was rare, but it happened in the young adult. We had done everything we could, we told the mother. But yet, there was no drug against the flu virus to save her son.

The raspy cough of Mr Król's broke my thoughts. The nurse was already unbuttoning the patient's pyjamas, speaking to him in a low soothing voice, 'Here we are, Mr Król. Doctor is going to examine you and then you'll get something for this nasty cough'.

Thirty minutes later, walking towards the staff room, I thought again about my own son. For the last few days his kindergarten had been closed. Every morning at seven o'clock, before coming to work, I had to take him to my parents, but tonight my mother was staying with him in my flat. When she arrived in the early morning, I could see she had been worrying. 'What's wrong Mum?' I asked.

'It's you and your hospital. You look so tired. I hope you don't catch anything nasty there. I pray you don't bring those viruses home to Stefan.' Her words were echoing in my head when I recalled one of my colleagues this morning saying that the Children's Hospital had a few toddlers with meningitis, associated with the flu. Oh, God, please keep my son safe, I sighed, overcoming a temptation to phone home immediately. Surely, if something was wrong, they would call me. I tried to calm myself down as I opened the door marked 'Doctor on Duty'.

Just as I collapsed on the couch the phone rang.

'Doctor, I'm the receptionist from the main entrance. I have some people with me. They are from the local television channel. They would like to talk to the doctor on duty.'

'Did they say what they want?'

'No. I have already told them we have had a terrible day here, but they still insist on seeing you.' Then she added in a whisper. 'They have cameras, lights, all their equipment with them.'

'All right, I'm coming down.' What else could I say? This was the last thing I needed just now. Television people, here!

On the way down the stairs my feet ached as much as my head. Then I saw them. A group of young people, wrapped up in warm clothes against the chilly rain of the late Polish November. There was a bohemian air about them. Somehow, they managed to look different from the everyday crowd on the street of this communist country. It was the way in which the colourful scarf was draped on the young woman's shoulders, the black French beret worn by one of the men, and the small backpack dotted with the foreign signs carried by the other.

And there I was, worn out, grey and heavy with tiredness, covered with layers of human emotion to the point of numbness.

The man holding the camera couldn't have been more than twenty-two. His cheeks were pink from the cold wind.

A fringe of wet hair hung over his eyes. He moved towards me, smiling.

'We are sorry, Doctor. We have already heard that you had a busy day.'

I listened without a word while he continued, 'This flu is a really bad one, but we would like to ask your permission for a few nice shots for tomorrow's news. What can you offer us Doctor?'

They all looked at me waiting.

'What can I offer?' I could hear anger in my voice. 'Look! The hospital is full to the brim. Yesterday we had to open another ward. Today stretchers are already filling the corridors. Half of our staff are sick!' I couldn't stop. 'Do you know that we have no more space in the morgue; there is a shortage of coffins in the city, and there are queues for funeral services?'

There was a long silence. Then the girl with a microphone in her hand and an expression of determination on her face said in a quiet voice, 'Yes, we know all that. We have been reporting these things for the last few nights. The whole city feels and looks like it must have been during the medieval plague. People are scared and depressed. We don't want to frighten them anymore.' She was now pleading, 'Can you please, give us something optimistic, something cheerful?'

Optimistic and cheerful. In this place. Now! It took me a moment to understand what she was saying. Then I realised. Yes, of course there was a place they could go. I was there early this morning when their registrar had asked me for a consultation. I was surprised to hear people laughing, joking and making plans for the future.

'All right, you may go to the seventh floor. The delivery ward is there. Tell them you have my permission.'

On the way back to my ward, listening again to the muffled sounds of sleeping misery around me, I thought, this night will soon end, and in the morning everything will look better. I smiled, seeing in my mind the young face of the cameraman. One day my son would be like him.

THE WEDGE

hammered early into our lives dividing bodies minds
working women with split personalities what comes
first Family or Work constant war which can't
be won battle after battle victories and
defeats no Nobel prize no medals for
stubbornness   bravery   sacrifices
wounds   injuries   difficult   to   heal
scars   for   ever   the   wedge
drives   further   in   an   empty
space   left   behind   is   filling
with   a   new   growth   guilt
that   thrives   on   failures
coming   from   both
sides   no   weapon
powerful   enough
to keep it under
control & life
goes on   till
we   retire
and   the
war   is
over
?

I Couldn't Do Anything

'Mum, can we go faster?' Stefan asked.

'No. I have to follow the speed limit,' I said.

We were on our way to Inowlodz. It was not far, about eighty kilometres along country roads. I looked briefly at my six-year-old son sitting next to me and I said, 'I'm sure your Grandma will walk to meet us somewhere on the way.'

'I would like to be there now,' Stefan said in his grumpy voice.

'We'll be there in an hour and a half. Don't sulk. It's such a beautiful day,' I said. We were already out of town, and I opened the sunroof. The smell of freshly ploughed soil mixed with a hint of smoke from burning potato stubble filled the car. 'We can have a little fire on the riverbank and bake a few potatoes,' I said watching the road in front of me.

'Great,' Stefan shouted and then he said, 'I'll pick up the wood and Grandpa will help me to make the fire. Can you go faster, Mum?'

'No. I can't. I'm doing seventy kilometres now and, on this road, I can't go faster, you should know that. We've driven here many times before.' Then I added, 'And we're not in a hurry. I've had enough of rushing around in the hospital during the last twenty-four hours.'

'There is no one on the road now,' Stefan murmured under his breath.

'Yes. That's good,' I said looking at the empty road in front of me and the warning sign of the bend coming up. I slowed down remembering this bend was too sharp to take in top gear. I knew that once through the bend there was a long stretch of straight road amongst the fields.

'Mum, a bird, look up there over that tree, it must be a hawk,' Stefan said excited.

But I didn't react. I watched the road. We drove out of the bend onto the straight and I was about to accelerate when in the distance I saw something dark lying in the middle of the road. I braked, changed gears and with caution drove towards it. Something was moving there. A few metres further and I realised that it was a motorbike lying in the middle of the road with one of its wheels spinning slowly in the air. I pulled over and switched off the engine.

'Stay here,' I said to Stefan. I jumped out and slammed the car door.

I ran to the middle of the road and stopped. A few metres from the motorbike lay a man, motionless and close to him a mangled bicycle. Another man, in a leather jacket, sat on the edge of the road. He held his head in his hands and repeated over and over like a mantra, 'I killed a man… I killed a man…' A third man lay in the grass on the side of the road. He was moving, trying to sit up.

For a few seconds I stood there and didn't know what to do. Then I hurried to the motionless man first. He was in his thirties, in country clothes. He was not breathing. Blood pooled around his injured head. There was no pulse, no heartbeat. I tried a short resuscitation but without success and gave up. He was dead and I couldn't do anything for him. I was still kneeling in the middle of the road when I heard a man's voice close to me. I looked up.

An old farmer, straddling a bicycle, stood behind me. 'I'll ride to the village to call an ambulance and the police,' he said and rode off.

I got up and rushed towards the man in the grass. He sat leaning backwards, supporting himself with his arms. His left leg was bent and the right extended but twisted inwards. The trousers over the right thigh were torn and there was a gash in the thigh, bleeding. It looked like his right leg was broken and there was trauma to the knee joint as well. His pulse was fast, blood pressure seemed okay. I quickly inspected the wound in his thigh and thought the bleeding was coming from torn muscles, not the major arteries. He was fully conscious. I asked him to lie down and not move, and then I hurried to the third man still sitting on the edge of the road, repeating his words like a continual lament, 'I killed a man...'

He was short and lightly built. I realised he must have been the man riding the motorbike. He was obviously in shock. I squatted next to him looking for any visible injuries. The left sleeve of his thick leather jacket was ripped open and his shirt sleeve, torn. It was soaked with blood. He was still wearing a helmet. I couldn't see his face covered by his palms. Both his bare hands had scratches and cuts.

'Do you feel pain anywhere?' I asked in a low voice while I lightly touched his right hand.

He didn't respond and continued his lament.

'I'm a doctor,' I said. 'You are injured. I need to check your wound.'

He didn't move. Still talking to him I tried to have a closer look at his arm when I heard the wail of the siren. It became louder and louder and then stopped. The sound of brakes squealing came together with a crunch of the gravel, and then silence fell over the road. I looked behind me. An ambulance was parked on the side of the road and a doctor was rushing towards me.

Thank God, I thought, I wasn't alone here anymore.

In the next few minutes, a second ambulance arrived followed by a police car. The ambulance crews got busy with the two injured men and the police wanted to ask me some questions. 'I have to go to my son first,' I said, and I turned towards our car.

The driver's door was ajar. Stefan stood behind it, his pale face next to the window, eyes wide open. He obviously had been watching me all the time.

'I'm coming,' I called and hurried towards him. I grabbed him in my arms and for a long moment we stood there without a word. Then I walked with him to the other side of the car. Still hugging him I sat in the passenger seat and tried to explain to him what had happened. He listened and interrupted me only once, 'Is the man,' he hesitated, 'the one lying on the road, dead?' he asked.

'Yes,' I said.

'You couldn't do anything?'

'No. But the two other men will be all right,' I said. 'You saw the ambulances. They are taking both men to the hospital.' I paused and still holding Stefan close to me I said, 'The police want to ask me a few questions and I – '

'Why?'

'Because we were the first ones to arrive here after that accident happened,' I said quietly and stroked Stefan's hair. 'I told the policeman, that one there,' I pointed to the man in a grey police uniform writing in his notebook, 'that after I talked to you, I'd answer his questions. I'd better go to him now and then we will be able to drive away from here.' I got up, but Stefan was still clinging to me. 'Please Stefan…. let me go, I won't be long,' I said, and gently released myself from his hands. 'And please, sit here, and wait for me. You can see me through the window.' I tried to smile, shut the car door, and walked to the policeman.

He took my particulars, asked a few questions about the accident, made a note of the address and the telephone of the pension where we were going to stay overnight and then I was free to leave.

Back in the car I smiled at Stefan and said, 'We can go now.' But I didn't move. I shut my eyes and sat there trying to calm myself. When after a few moments I finally placed my hands on the steering wheel they shook slightly, and my heart was still racing while I put the car into first gear. We drove slowly forward.

Stefan sat silently watching the road in front of us. I accelerated to forty kilometres an hour and changed to second gear when he said, 'Mum, don't go so fast, Mum.'

Pink Pyjamas

There was a knock at the door. 'Come in,' I called, and put the pen away.

It was Dorota, the nurse from the Cardiac Intensive Care Unit. She was twenty-four and pretty. With her plait of wheat-coloured hair and big blue eyes she could have posed for a portrait of a typical Slavic girl. Brisk in her manner in dealing with patients, she always won them over with a most disarming smile that showed her dimples.

'Doctor,' she said. 'You asked me to remind you to check on Mr Poleski at ten.'

'Yes, thank you. Wait a moment. How is he?' I asked and stood up looking at the table. 'My stethoscope...' I said.

'It's on your neck,' Dorota said with a short chuckle.

'Oh, right. Thanks, silly of me.' I touched the stethoscope thinking it had become like a part of my body, grown into it. We left the room together. 'And Mr Poleski?' I asked Dorota again.

'He is free of pain and his rhythm is okay. He is really well. Too well,' she said and she laughed before she added. 'A short time ago he just wanted to get up and walk to the toilet. I had to fight with him to convince him to pee into the bottle and have a bed pan when he needed to open his bowel. He was most upset, but finally I told him I would tie him to the bed if he didn't listen to me and do what I said.' She shook her head. 'Men,' she murmured under her breath when we entered the Unit.

From a distance I saw Mr. Poleski in his bed. He was fifty-six, an engineer, well built and fit. He had never been seriously ill before. Admitted with a heart attack, he had developed a rhythm problem. I had been worried about him and was monitoring him closely all day, not sure if he might need a pacemaker.

The patient smiled when he saw us coming towards him.

'How are you now?' I asked the patient.

'I'm fine, Doctor. Nothing wrong with me, really. I could get up and walk,' he said.

I examined him while Dorota attended to another patient. My examination confirmed what she had told me. The patient had improved markedly; his lungs were clear, and his heart rhythm was regular. As he had already come out of the most dangerous period I sighed with relief and hung the stethoscope back on my neck.

'You are a lot better,' I said to Mr Poleski. 'But you are not ready for a walk, not yet.'

'Doctor, please, only to the toilet,' he said in a begging tone. Then he leant towards me, lowered his voice and he added, 'I can't here…not now. In the morning there was an older nurse, grey hair… this one is so young and pretty… I'm so embarrassed, really, please Doctor…'

'You shouldn't be,' I said. I sat on the edge of his bed and for the next ten minutes I tried to explain to Mr Poleski that this was a part of our work, we were used to it, and he shouldn't feel ashamed in any way. 'You shouldn't worry about those things. You need to be in bed for your heart and this is the most important thing you should concentrate on now,' I said in conclusion.

Before I left, I asked Dorota to remind me to check on the patient in two hours time. On the way back I thought that severe pain and fear equalized us at the basic level of our existence but when they were gone our personalities showed up.

The ward was quiet, and I decided to get some sleep. After a quick shower I put on my favorite pink pyjamas with the top that looked like a short-sleeved shirt, and I went to bed.

Dorota's call woke me before one am. It took me only a moment to shake off sleep from my brain and get my mind fully alert. I put a white doctor's coat over my pyjamas and walked to the Cardiac Intensive Care Unit.

After talking to Dorota I checked on my patient. All was well. He was free of pain and stable. As I left him, he said, 'Thank you Doctor, I really feel good now. But Doctor' –

I was already two steps away from his bed. I stopped and turned back. 'Yes?' – I said.

He smiled. 'I have to say Doctor that pink suits you very well.'

I smiled automatically and for a long moment I stood there looking at my patient. Then, I shook my head and still smiling I turned and walked into the empty, dimly lit corridor filled with the usual hospital smells of diseases and bleach.

The Accident

'I'm going up to my ward,' I said to Krystyna, the petite nurse in the admission room.

'I hope it will be quiet now. We need a break,' Krystyna said as she spread the clean sheet over the examining couch.

I looked at the wall clock. It was five to two in the morning. Behind the window, the city night hung like a dirty-grey/purple rag. 'Keep your fingers crossed,' I said. 'My head seems full of lead. I'm dreaming about a cup of coffee and putting my feet up.'

I took the stethoscope from the table, hung it on my neck. and stretching my shoulders, I took a deep breath. My nostrils filled with the smell of stale sweat and the scent of chlorine from the hospital linen. 'I'd better move. I hope I don't see you too soon,' I said and grinned to Krystyna. As I turned to go, I heard running footsteps in the corridor. Krystyna frowned and looked at the door. A man burst into the room.

He stopped abruptly before us. 'There's been an accident, just in front of the hospital,' he shouted. Then he said to me, 'Doctor, come quickly…a man was hit by a motorbike… Doctor, hurry.'

Krystyna and I looked at each other.

'Call the ambulance,' I said to her.

'Doctor, you have to come!' He stepped closer to me.

There was urgency but also anger in his voice and I smelt the alcohol on his breath.

'Doctor, you–' he started.

'We will go,' I said quickly, 'but we need to call another doctor to stay here. I can't leave the hospital like this.' I turned to Krystyna, 'Get the first aid bag, torches and a stretcher; I'll phone the surgeon to come down.'

In a few minutes we were ready and carrying our load we followed the man. We rushed through the corridor towards the emergency entrance and out of the hospital. The man told us the accident had happened about five hundred metres away, on the other side of the street. It was two-way street divided by tramlines running in the middle. On the far side was a park, a well-known gathering place of drunks.

It was a moonless night, and the street had poor lighting. We crossed the footpath, then the street, empty at that time of night, and then with our stretcher we scrambled over the tramlines. The further we went from the hospital the darker it became. Finally, to the right, about a hundred metres ahead of us, at the edge of the road near the tramline, a small group was silhouetted. We heard angry shouts.

We negotiated the last part of the street and arrived at the group of about ten people standing in a circle. They gestured with their arms and shook their fists shouting, '…you killed him…'

'…you bloody bastard…'

'…you son of a bitch…'

The array words of swearing flowed into the night. They were getting louder as we walked closer.

'Let the doctor in, let her in,' our man yelled, pushing his way through the angry circle. The shouting died. An opening appeared, Krystyna and I moved in. The ring closed tight behind us.

In front of me on the street lay a body of a man in his forties, his head and shoulders covered in blood. I knelt next to him. The rough surface of the road bit into the skin of my knees. One close look at the man was enough for me to realise he was dead. In the light of Krystyna's torch, I briefly examined him. He had deep wound in the back of his head. There was no pulse and no heartbeat. There was nothing I could do for him.

The angry crowd watched my movements. I felt the close presence of their bodies, smelled the sweat and odour of unwashed clothes. The smell of alcohol wafted in and out.

I was bending over him during the examination and when I straightened for a moment somebody said, 'He is dead, isn't he?'

I said nothing.

The shouts and swearing were back, voices crossing over my head. There was some movement amongst the group. I looked up. To the left of me, a drunken bully grabbed a young man in a parka by the shoulders and was shaking him violently.

'You killed him, you son of a bitch, you...' the bully man shouted.

They are going to kill him – I thought, and I shivered, feeling the angry circle tighten, pushing closer around us. A moment of panic spread through me. I took a deep breath, and then I bent again over the dead man. I put the stethoscope to his chest.

'You men! Be quiet!' Krystyna yelled. 'The Doctor needs to hear.'

The noise around me decreased to a loud murmur. With both my hands I started pressing rhythmically on the dead man's chest, as if I was resuscitating him. And I prayed for the ambulance and police to come.

Then I heard the bell of the night tram. It came louder, the light of the tram illuminated our small group, and the tram stopped.

Within moments the tram driver, a tall sturdy man pushed his way through the crowd.

'Let him go,' he said loudly and tried to pull away the bully holding the motorbike rider. Then all the voices were drowned out in the wailing of sirens, that grew louder and louder and stopped. Car brakes screeched and when I turned towards the noise, I saw the ambulance doctor and his driver run towards us. They were followed by two police officers.

The doctor looked at me. I shook my head. He nodded and then squatted next to the body lying between us.

I stood up feeling dizzy. My legs seemed made of dough.

'Can we go now?' Krystyna asked.

'I think that the police want a word with me,' I said, as I noticed one of the policemen striding over.

He took our names and before he let us go, he said, 'Doctor, when we are finished here, we need a few details from you. It shouldn't take too long.'

'You know where you can find us,' I said.

Krystyna took the bag, we found our torches and carrying the stretcher we started the slow walk back to the hospital. A few metres on we passed another policeman questioning the motorbike rider. I heard the young man's trembling voice saying, 'I saw him at the last moment… he appeared from nowhere…jumped onto the road…straight in front of me… he must have been drunk…I couldn't stop…couldn't do anything…'

Hippocratic Oath

On the 6th of October 1939 the Polish Army, fighting against the German forces since the 1st of September, was defeated. Germany and the Soviet Union gained full control over Poland.

'I was attached to the military hospital. I was supposed to treat the sick and to help with sorting out the incoming wounded, but after our defeat I found myself as the only doctor in a field hospital full of wounded Polish soldiers. A German officer was placed in charge of the hospital,' Dad said, and paused, as we heard my mother coming into the room. She brought tea and a platter with rhubarb pie.

'It's still warm and I even have some cream for it,' she said taking her place. 'What have you been talking about?' she asked serving the pie.

'Dad's fighting at the beginning of the war.'

'I had a gun, but I wasn't fighting. I was there to save lives, not to kill people, as I had pledged in my Hippocratic Oath. But...' Dad shook his head, 'I know that I killed some of those poor wounded, even if I tried to do my best treating them,' he said. He pushed aside his plate of cake, took up his pipe and started to fill it with tobacco. I watched his fingers moving in a steady, measured way to perform their task. They were doctor's fingers, sensitive, yet firm in their grip. He lit the pipe and after a few puffs he continued:

'Many of those injured needed to be operated on immediately. I cleaned and sewed the open wounds, set the fractures, and tried to comfort those dying from fatal injuries to the head, chest, and abdomen. But there were several soldiers with wounds to their limbs. Those men needed amputations. Some had developed gangrene already.' Dad paused and puffed his pipe. He looked at me, 'I was a physician and had never done an amputation before, but there was no surgeon. Also, our dressing material and drugs, particularly anaesthetics and analgesics, were running out, but the time for those wounded was running out as well.'

Dad sighed and stopped. When he started to speak again, he was not looking at us. He was obviously back in the tent of that makeshift hospital. 'The nurse,' he said, 'held an anatomy book in front of me as I operated. We used the rest of our alcohol supply as an anaesthetic, and when that finished, I operated and prayed for those men to lose consciousness from the pain.'

'War,' my mother said, 'There is nothing worse than that.'

'You are right. I'm sure I'll never forget it.' Dad was silent for a long moment and before he spoke again something like a smile moved his lips. 'One night, just after midnight, the German officer, the hospital commandant, came to my tent. He looked around as if making sure I was alone and then took out of his pocket a small package. "I brought you some morphine. I shouldn't. Don't tell anyone," he said. And before he left, he added, 'I'm a doctor, too."'

'He was obviously still human, but you couldn't say that about many of them later,' my mother said.

'No, you couldn't,' Dad said in a voice we could hardly hear and then he started to empty his pipe that stopped burning long before.

*   *   *

On the 8th of October 1939 Germany and the Soviet Union divided Poland. Germany annexed the western part of the country and the Free City of Danzig; the Soviet Union annexed eastern Poland. The remaining Polish territory Germany placed under the administration of a newly formed General Government.

'After the end of the 39 campaign I came home to Lodz. It was already a part of Germany and the mass repressions against Polish citizens had started. The Germans allowed us to work, but to treat only Poles,' Dad said to Witold, his old friend from the Warsaw Medical School. They had lost contact during the war, and now, in nineteen forty-nine they met again and were catching up on the events of those past years.

'Witold sighed and took a sip of brandy.' I was captured in Vilnius by Russians,' he said, 'but I escaped, came to Warsaw, and joined the underground army. Through our contacts we knew exactly what was going on in Lodz. After a short time, my friends had found me a job in a hospital where I worked as a surgeon, and, in that hospital, we saved the lives of a good number of our members injured in action.'

Dad put down his glass. 'After my return to Lodz, I got back to my old hospital, but we expected it to be closed at any time. They had already arrested Dr Wender, the medical director, and Professor Pilski, the head of the surgical unit. I just waited for my turn to come any minute.'

'Being a doctor didn't help us then. Just the opposite, it was a reason to get us killed.'

'Yes, as the professionals we were high on the Germans' extermination list. But…' Dad smiled and drank from his glass before he continued. 'I was lucky and just once, it was my profession that saved my life.'

I knew the story, but I was listening to Dad, as if I was hearing it for the first time, when he said, 'One night long after the curfew there was a knock on the front door. You can imagine,' Dad lifted his eyebrows and grinned to Witold. 'Of course, I thought, this time it was for me. I opened the door and saw a young Gestapo Officer. He said, he had heard I was a doctor, and a good one, and he wanted me to see his sick sister. I said I couldn't do this because, as he must know, I wasn't allowed to treat Germans. He said he was aware of it, but he was just ordering me to go with him and see his sister.'

Dad paused for a short time and continued, 'We went to his flat. His sister was a sixteen-year-old girl. When I looked at her, at that very moment, she was my patient, like any others before, and at her bed I was just a doctor doing my job. I examined her. She had scarlet fever. He walked me back home. I had to see her a few more times. As we both know,' Dad nodded to Witold, 'there was no treatment for scarlet fever then, just aspirin, but fortunately she recovered fully. At the last visit he thanked me, and I thought that was the end of it. But a few weeks later, he came late in the evening and said, 'Your name is on the list of arrests for tonight. You need to leave your flat, now.' And he was gone.'

Dad took another sip of his brandy. 'In no time, I grabbed some documents, hidden gold coins, and my late mother's jewellery. I put it all into my pockets, got my coat and left. In a few days, with the help of some friends, I crossed the so called "Green Border" to the General Government, and for the rest of the war I lived in a small village in a ranger's house.'

'You were lucky,' Witold said turning his glass and watching the oily film the brandy made. Then he said, 'They were unpredictable. Sometimes it could be just their good or bad humour that made a difference between life and death.'

Dad nodded. 'I know. A few weeks after my escape, I received a message from my housekeeper that they had come that night looking for me. They arrested several of my friends and colleagues. Some were killed in jail, some ended up in concentration camps, only a few survived.'

Witold shook his head. 'We both were lucky,' he said. He put down his glass and looked at his watch. He got up. 'I'd better go. My train to Warsaw is in forty minutes.'

Dad got up as well, and they walked together to the hall. I heard Dad saying, 'I hope you may visit us again when you come to Lodz. It is always good, even if it is sad, to talk about that time, and remember our colleagues.'

*　*　*

Ten minutes before the end of my dad's surgery hours the bell rang at our front door. I left my Latin textbook on the desk and went to answer. I saw a tall man in his forties with dark blond hair and blue eyes, narrowed by heavy eyelids. He was clutching the right side of his abdomen. He apologised for coming late and without an appointment, but he hoped the doctor could still see him this evening.

'You need to talk to the doctor yourself,' I said and let the man in. I gestured to one of the chairs in the hall. 'Please wait here. The doctor won't be too long,' I said and went back to the translation of *Caesar's* letter.

It was six-thirty that evening, when I finished my school homework. I took my book and went looking for Dad. He was in the study packing his doctor's bag.

'Do you have a home visit?' I said.

'Yes. Do you need me now?'

'I just finished my Latin, and I wondered if you could check it,' I said.

'We will do it when I come back,' Dad said.

He put the stethoscope into the bag as Mum came in.

126

'You'd better hurry up with your visit. We don't want to eat too late,' she said to Dad and then she added. 'That last patient took you a long time.'

'I think he has a stone in his kidney. He was in a lot of pain. I had to give him an injection and wait till his pain eased.'

I listened to Dad with my full attention, interested as always in everything related to his medical practice. It was my dream to become a doctor.

'Basia, you saw that patient, didn't you?' Dad's question broke my thoughts.

'Yes.'

'What did you think about him?'

'What do you mean? There was nothing special about him except he appeared very anxious to see you, obviously because of his pain.'

'Yes, he looked ordinary, but when after examining his abdomen, I asked him to sit up and take his shirt off, he hesitated before he did. And then as I put my stethoscope to his chest, I saw it, the blood group tattooed under his left arm.'

We all knew what it meant. The war had ended three years ago, and its horror was still fresh in our minds. I was a child when it started, but still, in that long moment of silence that followed Dad's words, the scenes from the past flashed through my brain bringing back the men in hated uniforms with SS insignia. Finally, it was my mother who said it. 'The man was in the Gestapo.' Her voice was quiet, but every word perfectly heard. She frowned and looking at Dad with her eyes wide open she asked, 'And what now? What are you going to do?'

Dad's gaze wandered from Mum to me and then went back to Mum. He shook his head. 'Nothing', he said.

'Nothing…' Mum repeated as if she wanted to be sure of the meaning of the word.

'He came to me as a patient, and I treated him as I would treat any other of my patients. That's all,' Dad said.

He put the prescription pad into his doctor's bag and shut the clasp. 'I need to go. I don't want to be late,' he said. He gave Mum a kiss and left the room.

Quiet Funeral

'We should notify the newspaper,' my mother said. She looked at me, waiting. Her eyes were red, lids swollen, the usual sparks of laughter gone. On her pale face, sleepless nights wrote their signs.

'You are right we should. I haven't thought about it,' I said. 'If we write it now and I take it to the editorial office straight away it will be published on Wednesday, two days before the funeral.' I tried to keep my voice steady, but I couldn't stop my tears.

'I want a quiet funeral, just our closest family.' My mother's voice broke my thoughts. 'You know how much your dad hated a big crowd.'

'We can't avoid it. So many people in this town know him – knew him', I corrected myself. 'It was his town. He loved the place, he always came back here', I said. 'There must have been thousands of people who Dad met in his working life as a doctor. He remembered many of his patients, and I'm sure most of his patients would remember him.'

'He loved his work.' My mother's hand smoothed the piece of blank paper that lay on the table in front of her. She sighed, pushed the page and pen towards me, 'You write it, I can't.' She hesitated, 'If we can't avoid people coming to the cemetery, at least in the note we can ask them not to give condolences to the family at the funeral. I don't want to talk to anyone there.'

'Yes, we will do that,' I said.

We were half-way through our writing when the front doorbell rang. I opened the door to see two men in tram workers' uniforms. The taller one had grey hair and kind dark eyes set deep in wrinkles. The other one was in his twenties, his uniform looked very new.

The older man bowed a little and said, 'Good morning. Could we speak to Doctor Kopczynski's wife?' When I hesitated, he added, 'We are from the City Trams. He was our doctor for the last eight years. We were very sorry to hear from our nurse that the Doctor died.'

I stood back two steps, 'I'm his daughter. Please come in. I'll tell my mother.'

When I explained to my mother who the people were, she sighed and with great reluctance went to the hall. After a few minutes she returned, turning her head in a gesture of disbelief and frustration.

'I don't know what to do,' she said. 'They are from the City Trams' band; they are asking my permission to play at the funeral. They said they want to walk with their doctor on his last journey.' She looked at me with her dark eyes full of tears which she tried to hold back. 'What are we going to do?'

We looked at each other. We both knew the band, an ensemble of about twenty men with their brass instruments. We had seen and heard them many times marching on the streets during official parades to celebrate the Russian Revolution's anniversary or the International Labour Day.

I broke the silence. 'We can't say no,' I said. 'They want to do it from the goodness of their heart.'

'I know, but I can't – 'my mother sat heavily on the chair next to the table and started to sob.

'We will get through it, together,' I put my arms around her shaking shoulders. 'Stay here,' I said. 'I'll thank them and tell them that we appreciate their offer, and we know their doctor would like it.'

When on the day of the funeral we arrived at the cemetery, we saw a crowd of people in front of the chapel. The band was already there visible from a distance. In their dark blue formal uniforms, the men stood silently in two rows alongside the path leading to the chapel. The big trombones polished like mirrors caught the late morning sun filtered through the young leaves of the chestnut and maple trees.

After a short service we followed the coffin to its resting place. The sound of Chopin's Funeral March filled the alley, hung among the old trees, and drifted towards the blue sky. My mother held her tears, but I couldn't stop crying. In my mind I saw Dad sitting at the piano, his long fingers moving over the black and white keys. He looked at me and smiled.

Acknowledgments

My gratitude goes first to my parents and my stepfather. During difficult times in communist Poland, they nurtured me as a child and supported me through my studies and my early medical career.

I thank all who taught me, my professors, my colleagues, my friends.

Above all, I am grateful to my patients, who taught me about life.

I wrote these stories after coming to live in Australia, with the encouragement of my Australian friends especially Trevor Code and Brian Edwards from the Deakin Literary Society. Brian's work in editing this book was invaluable.

This thank you extends to my writer friends in Port Macquarie, who supported me through this journey.

The Canadian writer Barbara Turner-Vesselago inspired me with her freefall teaching.

Special thanks go to my daughter-in-law, Joanna, who painted the artwork featured on the cover. To all my family, these are your stories too.

About the Author

Barbara Orłowska-Westwood was born in Poland and migrated to Australia in 1979. A physician, now retired, she worked in her profession in both countries. In retirement, she enjoys writing poetry and prose and her writing has been published in Australia, Poland and America. A chapbook of her poetry Firing Neurons was published by PressPress in 2010. Her second book, Living Lines Are Never Straight, was published in 2020.